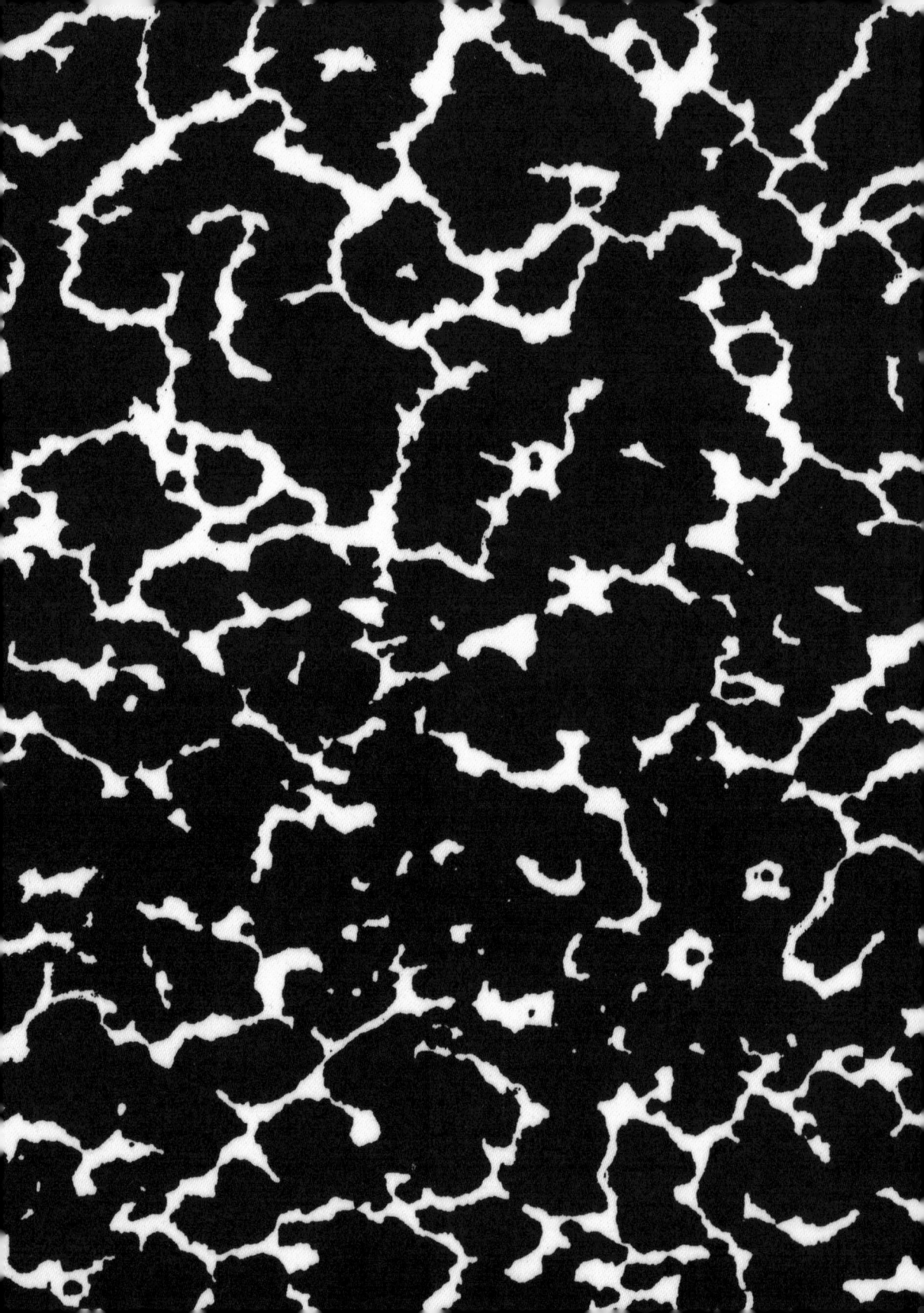

ROBERT VENTURI, DENISE SCOTT BROWN, AND STEVEN IZENOUR AT ACADIA SUMMER ARTS PROGRAM

by Marion Boulton Stroud

Essay by Kathryn Bloom Hiesinger
Designed by Takaaki Matsumoto

Acadia Summer Arts Program

Published by Acadia Summer Arts Program

Marion Bolton Stroud, Publisher
Takaaki Matsumoto, Matsumoto Incorporated, New York,
Producer and Designer
Amy S. Wilkins, Editor and Manager of Publications

Printed and bound by Nissha Printing Co., Ltd., Kyoto, Japan

Cover, end leaves: Notebook fabric by Venturi, Scott Brown and
Associates for the Fabric Workshop and Museum, Philadelphia, 1983

Cover illustration: Drawing by Venturi, Scott Brown and Associates
of front elevation of Deer Acres structures. From left to right: Temple
shed, Flower tent, Palette house, and T-shirt house

Page 8: Map of Mount Desert Island, Maine, June 1893

Photography Credits:
Robert Addman: 12 left; Will Brown: 13–16, 17 right, 18–19, 41, 71,
76–79, 81, 87–91, 96–99; Courtesy A.S.A.P.: 21 right, 22; Courtesy
Edgar Heap of Birds: 20; Courtesy the Fabric Workshop and
Museum: 12 right; Courtesy Son of the South: 8; Courtesy Venturi,
Scott Brown and Associates: 24–25, 29, 37, 102–3; David Graham:
21 left, 23, 59, 64–65; Frank Hanswijk: 11 left, 11 middle; Steven
Izenour: 50–53, 62–63 bottom, 68; Story Litchfield: 26–27, 42–43,
72–73, 82–83; Julie Marquart: 11 right, 17 left; Takaaki Matsumoto:
62–63 top; Eugene Mopsick: 10; Matt Wargo: 54–57, 66–67, 69,
92–95, 101, 104–7, 111–13, 117–21.

Library of Congress Control Number: 2010901841
ISBN: 978-0-9797642-2-6

Available through D.A.P./Distributed Art Publishers
155 Sixth Avenue, 2nd Floor
New York, New York 10013
Tel: (212) 627.1999
Fax: (212) 627.9484
www.artbook.com

CONTENTS

"ISN'T LIFE A FACADE?"—ROBERT VENTURI

BY MARION BOULTON STROUD

Many of my fondest memories revolve around architecture and architects. My love of architecture is tied to my close attachment to my grandmother, Marion Sims Rosengarten. She and my grandfather, Frederic Rosengarten, had their home—which became my chosen residence for the first decades of my life—designed and built in 1929 by her beloved and talented brother, Joseph Patterson Sims. He was a principal of the venerable Philadelphia architectural firm of Willing, Sims, and Talbutt. My grandmother and grandfather's Philadelphia fieldstone home on Chestnut Hill Avenue overlooking Fairmount Park, named Indian Rock, was a most splendid space; double cube, large-windowed, and had an acoustically perfect, one thousand-square-foot ballroom-living room to which the renowned conductor of the Philadelphia Orchestra Leopold Stokowski brought quartets of his musicians to play. James B. Garrison's book *Houses of Philadelphia: Chestnut Hill and the Wissahickon Valley 1880–1930* noted that "Rarely does any house succeed in so perfectly reflecting the tastes, character, and achievements of its accomplished owner/occupants." Also, our "uncle George Howe," principal of Howe and Lescaze, (married to my much older cousin Maritje Patterson Howe) designed the country's first International Style skyscraper, the Philadelphia Savings Fund Society (PSFS) building (1929–32). He was a great Philadelphian modernist architect who was head of the Yale School of Architecture in the early 1950s.

Louis I. Kahn, who worked with Howe and Lescaze at the start of his career, could often be seen walking down our street on Sundays to visit Harriet Patterson and their son Nathaniel Kahn. I also worked for Margaret Esherick during the period in which she and Lou Kahn were designing her house on Pastorius Park in Chestnut Hill. As a graduate student in art history at the University of Pennsylvania, I loved to give tours of the three houses built for single women in a two-mile radius by Louis I. Kahn, Robert Venturi, and Romaldo Giurgola. I learned to think about architecture by quoting Kahn's philosophy: "What does a building want to be?" Forty years later, as part of the Acadia Summer Arts Program (A.S.A.P.), I was delighted to be able to invite Nathaniel Kahn to screen the film he made about his father, *My Architect*, which was nominated for an Academy Award as the best documentary feature.

As I came to know the principals of Philadelphia's next great architectural firm, Robert

Venturi, Denise Scott Brown, and Steve Izenour, of Venturi, Scott Brown and Associates (VSBA), we used different language about buildings, including "make it bigger, make it better;" "we build from the inside out;" "less is more is a bore," and as Bob often says, "isn't life a facade?" I first got to know the Venturi–Scott Brown family on a personal level quite by accident as we boarded the same plane to London. While Bob waved goodbye, I helped Denise carry on their new son, Jimmy, along with all his baby paraphernalia. My dear friends Anne d'Harnoncourt and her husband, Joe Rishel, encouraged me to invite Bob and Denise to my family house in Northeast Harbor, Maine for a long weekend. VSBA had already designed a shingle-style house on Mount Desert Island for one of my childhood friends. They were charming and appreciative houseguests. When we returned to Philadelphia I got up the nerve to invite them to design repeat yardage to be produced at the Fabric Workshop. The staff and I were absolutely thrilled when they accepted our offer, and produced the now signature fabric patterns, Notebook and Grandmother (Granny). From the fabrics, the firm went on to design the Fabric Workshop and Museum's new space at 1315 Cherry Street. They sent their strong and invaluable right arm, Steve Izenour, to the rescue. In exchange for "two dogs and a Coke," "Steve Ize," as we called him, designed our galleries, print tables, lunch room, offices, and archives.

I met many of the talented specialists associated with VSBA, including Tim Kearney, Claudia Cueto, Steve's son John Izenour, and Lauren Jacobi. I also met Michael Wommack of Michael Wommack Studios, an incredibly talented colorist, for airbrush painting, signage, and color match, and Steve Schultz of Electro Mechanical Systems, a genius at bending and cutting metal, for fabricating outdoor metal signage and facades. They all worked with the Fabric Workshop and Museum, and later at A.S.A.P./Kamp Kippy on Mount Desert Island. I also consulted on designs for A.S.A.P. with other architects and friends, including John Lucas of KPF, Richard Gluckman, Liz Diller, and Ric Scofidio in New York; John Vinci in Chicago; and Frank Gehry and Edwin Chan and the artist Jorge Pardo in California.

The most fun I've had over the years has been not just thinking about architecture, but actually renovating and building on the different properties purchased in Maine for A.S.A.P./ Kamp Kippy. Bob, Denise, and their partner, my dear, departed friend and iconoclastic genius, Steve, were my principal architects. If Steve often called Bob and Denise "Ma" and "Pa,"(I called them "God" and "Goddess") I thought of Steve as a brother—a muscular daredevil who loved physical challenges, like riding a collapsible, portable bicycle twenty-four miles from Franklin, Maine to Indian Point Road, fearlessly sailing across the Atlantic, and displacing tons of water whenever he dove into a pool—thereafter to be nicknamed the "Big Tuna." While Steve ordered his two dogs and a Coke for lunch in Philadelphia, in Maine he invariably ordered the hearty "Walking Boss" sandwich from Mother's Kitchen, made with beef, potatoes, and caramelized onions. Steve practically invented the popular use of Day-Glo greenish yellow and often wore clothes with this high-visibility hue later associated with school crossings and other safety zones. When Steve cycled from Franklin to Indian Point Road on Mount Desert, his Day-Glo parka was accessorized with aerodynamic sunglasses, complete with rearview mirrors on either side.

Steve was also a dreamer, with totally impossible, impractical, brilliant ideas. For A.S.A.P., Steve's first projects were temporary structures in his favorite shades of glowing blue and bright yellow—a blue cook shack to serve dinner guests and a bright yellow tent for lectures. However, the cook shack lacked ventilation—it fried the cooks—while the tent seriously leaked water and attracted moths and mosquitoes. Steve also invented an Ektachrome slide projector booth to keep the projectors quiet during lectures. It was wonderful to look at but totally unusable and totally in keeping with his character. To reward Steve for his heroic efforts over the cook shack and the tent, I went along with his proposal to build one of the most useless buildings ever designed, the "A-frame for Art." Like the cook shack and tent, it was quite beautiful to look at, but nearly impossible to inhabit, due to the heat generated by the traditional Maine ventorama windows Steve had installed. In VSBA fashion, Steve made the extraordinary out of the ordinary, a folly that has become one of the most photographed buildings on Mount Desert Island. Steve also designed the A.S.A.P. renovations to the old New England farmhouse and barn at Deer Acres, as well as their additions, the T-shirt house and Palette house, and lastly the green Flowers tent, decorated with orange, red and white flowers that glowed in the dark.

Together Steve and I learned the island's building codes by trial and error, with hundreds of phone calls and letters from the town of Bar Harbor and the National Park Service, telling us "you can't." As A.S.A.P./Kamp Kippy developed, I wanted some things to be systemized, but others to remain mystical. I didn't always know and couldn't always anticipate all the needs of the program. Projects like the Palette house addition got delayed until I could be satisfied that all their needs were being met. A lot of what we accomplished was based on intuition and bright ideas. Throughout, Steve kept his sense of humor. He had named the doors at the Fabric Workshop "In" for the entrance and "Out" for the exit; the A.S.A.P. outhouses were called "His" and "Hers." This "his" and "hers" division was emblematic of our enjoyable working relationship: I personally favored New England farmhouses with their outbuildings and simple Shaker and rural New England styles, the "big house, little house, back house, barn," while Steve continued to "Learn from Las Vegas" (and the decorated shed) and celebrate the vernacular of the highway. Bob and Denise came up to visit and lecture and were our wise sounding board, interjecting reason and planning into some of the more farfetched ideas.

Steve was on his way over from Vermont to show me his finalized designs for the big lecture tent when he suddenly died of an aneurism. After his unexpected, wrenching death, work on the Maine projects slowed down for a while as we all mourned his loss. Finally we got some momentum back and built the tent without him. In 2002, Bob and Denise came up to visit Maine again and lecture at A.S.A.P. They helped restart the planning process in grand style, by adding the facade to Steve's unfinished Palette house. Bob changed the color of the palette ornament from Steve's primary red, yellow and blue, (with a pink tube of paint breaking through the roofline), to Bob's very subtle camouflage colors, which reflected beautifully in the pond. Replacing Steve's temporary tent, Bob came to the rescue and finished the building by putting a gallery and reception room upstairs and a recreation room downstairs for cocktails and children's dining.

My wonderful Maine contractor, John Dargis, and his right hand man, John Albee, say that we are almost out of space for more additions at the Deer Acres site. Never able to take no for an answer, I've challenged them to find another site for new projects. We are still planning to add new structures that further embrace VSBA's aesthetic within the "VSBA Village." A.S.A.P./Kamp Kippy still needs a media center and I am committed to building Bob's "Big House/Little House" design that we have always wanted. And then there are the Billings farm and Town Hill Studios, which are still begging for VSBA designs of their own.

Balancing my love for unadorned New England farmhouse vernacular and Steve's and VSBA's drive for wild colors, embellishments, and historic references, we have the best of worlds, a collision of complexity and contradiction and the ordinary and the extraordinary. My architectural escapades have enshrined and made good neighbors of all-American farm buildings with an exotic A-frame guesthouse that everyone wants to photograph, but no one wants to spend the night in. I have wanted to unite vernacular and postmodern architecture and for rural New England structures to cohabitate with an homage that mixes up the Philadelphia Museum of Art, the Parthenon, and Venturi Scott Brown's Best Products floral facade. My lifelong devotion to architecture and architects has been learned no less from establishment Philadelphia than glitzy Las Vegas and down east Maine.

MAP
OF
MOUNT DESERT ISLAND
MAINE

Compiled for the
Flora of Mt. Desert Island

Scale
Statute Miles

Topography adapted from the
United States Coast Survey.
Figures on hills denote heights in feet.
Curves of equal elevation are given for
every 20 ft. difference in level. Datum is
High Water Mark.
Mean low water mark is shown by a
dotted line.
Nomenclature based on the most
trustworthy authorities.
June 1893

ROBERT VENTURI, DENISE SCOTT BROWN, AND STEVEN IZENOUR AT ACADIA SUMMER ARTS PROGRAM

BY KATHRYN BLOOM HIESINGER

Maine

The work of Venturi, Scott Brown and Associates (VSBA) is hardly uncharted territory: its principal architects are themselves prolific and talented writers. Nevertheless, the unique relationship that developed over three decades between the principals of the firm—Robert Venturi, Denise Scott Brown, and the late Steven Izenour—and Marion Boulton Stroud, known to all as "Kippy," has remained unchronicled until now, though distinguished for its duration, variety of projects undertaken, and utter loyalty on both sides. Out of the relationship has come fabric patterns, the graphic decoration of a stairwell, custom furniture and accessories, three exhibitions, a storefront window design, and the seven buildings that house the Acadia Summer Arts Program (A.S.A.P.) on Mount Desert Island, Maine. These buildings are the focus of this book, their design and decoration informed by the other projects Stroud and VSBA accomplished together. "Together" is an operative word in this ongoing architect–client relationship. Stroud is a knowledgeable client with a lifelong interest in architecture. In addition, she and Izenour learned to negotiate decisions as Stroud's programmatic needs changed, often more than once, over the course of a project.

The most important body of work realized by VSBA for Stroud are the buildings in Maine, and Maine is where she first met Robert Venturi and Denise Scott Brown. Stroud spent all of her childhood summers in her grandparents' large shingle-style house in the village of Northeast Harbor on Mount Desert Island, hiking in Acadia National Park, sailing among the islands that dot the coast, and making pine pillows when it rained. Her attachment to Mount Desert Island in general and her grandparents' house in particular is fierce, and Stroud was elated when she was able to buy the property after her mother's death. From the 1970s, she organized wonderful house parties over Labor Day weekend to share the pleasures of Mount Desert, her guests drawn largely from the art world of Philadelphia—curators from the Philadelphia Museum of Art (where she had worked in the mid-1960s) and artists and staff members of the Fabric Workshop and Museum (FWM) which Stroud founded in 1977 and where she continues to serve as artistic director. Sometime in the late 1970s (no one remembers the date), Anne d'Harnoncourt, then curator of twentieth-century art (and later director) at the Philadelphia

Marion Boulton Stroud

Museum of Art, suggested to Stroud that she invite Venturi and Scott Brown to Maine. The summer weekend they shared was a great success, leading to their first collaborative project, the development in 1982–83 of Venturi's Grandmother and Notebook fabric patterns at the FWM. Stroud offered VSBA the assistance of her technical staff of master printers, assistant printers, and construction technicians in creating prototypes that were hand-printed on cotton sateen. At the same time, VSBA's Flowers pattern, drawn from Venturi's 1977 facade design for the Best Products Company showroom in Langhorne, Pennsylvania, was studied by VSBA and the FWM, also printed on fabric as a prototype, but never put into production like Grandmother and Notebook. An all-over floral design, Flowers paralleled VSBA's increasing commitment to patterned surfaces in its architecture of the 1970s. Steven Izenour was involved marginally in the Grandmother, Notebook, and Flowers experiments at the FWM, and met Stroud through them, beginning a professional association and deep friendship that lasted until his untimely death in 2001. Like Stroud, Izenour was also deeply attached to Maine, spending many summers in a nineteenth-century farmhouse in Franklin, Maine, that belonged to his wife's family. He often visited Stroud, riding his bicycle the twenty-four miles between Franklin and Northeast Harbor.

During the 1980s, Stroud found that the occasional weekend wasn't enough to satisfy her interest in spending more time in Maine or to accommodate the increasing numbers of artists and friends she invited to join her. She began to rent and buy properties all over the island, beginning in 1989 with the purchase of a shingled shorefront cottage in Seal Cove overlooking Blue Hill Bay. Coincidentally, Venturi undertook a residential commission on Mount Desert in Seal Harbor from 1986 to 1989, its design reminiscent of traditional shingle-style cottages, its detail provided by local craftsmen in native stone and woods. When the house was completed in 1989, Venturi and Scott Brown invited Stroud to the opening.

The schedule of summer guests and activities that Stroud maintained on Mount Desert was formalized in 1993 as A.S.A.P., an invitation-only resident fellowship for artists and arts professionals who meet communally to share their work. The functions of administration, meeting, and dining for A.S.A.P. required a central site, and to that purpose, Stroud acquired

Robert Venturi

Denise Scott Brown

Steven Izenour

property in the neighborhood of Bar Harbor, from late 1993 through the spring of 1996, that sloped upward from Northwest Cove to the other side of Indian Point Road. A shingle-style house built in 1965 on the shores of Northwest Cove, Shore Cottage, became A.S.A.P.'s first home, while an old farmhouse across rural Indian Point Road, Deer Acres, renovated and expanded, now serves the same purpose. The previous owners had placed a conservation easement on the property with Acadia National Park, limiting land use, among other criteria, to single family residential structures. All of the building renovation and expansion designed by VSBA, therefore, had to comply with these restrictions.

As A.S.A.P. began to take shape, Stroud asked Venturi to design a building for her in Maine, "something he wanted to do," perhaps an unbuilt design—and assumed that she would "find the program afterward."[1] Stroud's open-ended invitation to Venturi was similar to that she offered artists-in-residence at the FWM, where she was willing to support the artists in whatever project they chose to pursue. With ongoing work ranging from the Hotel Mielmante Nikko Kirifuri in Nikko, Japan (1992–97) to various buildings for the Walt Disney World Resort in Florida (1992–98), Venturi had little time to consider another project in Maine, and instead gave responsibility for it to Izenour, who was already designing a floor plan for the FWM's new home at 1315 Cherry Street in Philadelphia. In 1995 a "professional relationship" was established between Stroud and VSBA, but not until 2002 was that relationship—until then based on "mutual understandings"—acknowledged and formalized with a written contract defining the firm's scope of architectural services as "design consultants, providing design drawings to your contractor."[2]

In 1995 Stroud mounted the first of two exhibitions of Izenour's work she would present at the FWM. "Signs of Fun: The Design Scrapbook of Steven Izenour," explored the sources of Izenour's inspiration, his favorite projects, and philosophy: "The Continuing Education of the Architect—from Las Vegas to Disney by way of VSBA." In an introductory text panel, he wrote:

> To be a halfway skillful architect in the late-twentieth century, you have to be willing to listen (to) and learn … all the time! … it is as important to see, appreciate, and learn from the everyday American landscape as it is to learn from the great

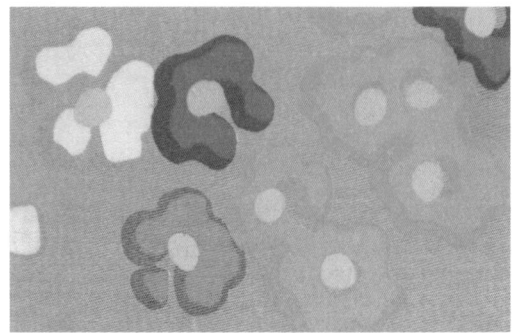

Robert Venturi and Denise Scott Brown with Queen Anne (left) and Empire (right) chairs for Knoll International (1978–84). Scott Brown is wearing a dress of Grandmother fabric, produced at the Fabric Workshop and Museum (FWM), Philadelphia (1983).

Flowers fabric by Venturi, Scott Brown and Associates (VSBA) for the FWM, 1982. Opposite: Stairwell connecting the fifth and sixth floors of the FWM, 1315 Cherry Street, Philadelphia, decorated with variant of Flowers pattern by Steven Izenour, 1998. This visibly false "wallpaper" is actually an appliqué: each flower is realized as a three-dimensional object attached to the wall.

> monuments of architectural history . . . architecture is a collaborative art, you
> need clients, partners, and fellow workers as mutual critics and for inspiration . . .
> While architecture is a serious business (you have to use someone else's money
> to do it), you should not take yourself too seriously—responsible design need not
> and should not be devoid of humor—have fun, it's the best revenge!

Izenour designed the exhibition at the FWM, transforming the entire gallery space into a colorful airbrushed landscape of grass and sky, with yellow road stripes on the floor to give direction, and large graphics in receding font sizes to suggest distance on the walls—Venturi, Scott Brown, and Izenour's Las Vegas landscape of "big spaces" and "high speeds"[3] viewed from the automobile. Drawings, photographs, and models were installed among signs and bulletin-board panels artfully crammed with images and source material, evoking the "messy vitality" so promoted and appreciated by the three architects. As Izenour described in another text panel titled with Venturi's aphorism, "Main Street is Almost All Right:" " . . . we can change the built environment . . . reveling in a complex, pluralistic environment juxtaposing signs, symbols and buildings of different styles and sizes."

Izenour's work in Maine for Stroud made its debut at this exhibition, notably, his "A-frame for Art/Kamp Kippy" and two "barn" studios ("1" and "2"), exhibited alongside postcard photographs of a real Maine barn with a similar roof treatment and weather vane, traditional farm sheds, and a boat building, illustrating the direct influence of these vernacular structures on the proposals. The barns were designed (but never built) in a traditional, straightforward style updated with a handsome clerestory of windows to serve the artist's studio inside. In "Signs of Fun," Izenour collaborated for the first time with his son, John Izenour, who had recently joined VSBA as collections manager, and in that capacity, introduced Photoshop production to the firm for the first time with this project. Izenour's other important collaborator was Michael Wommack, a painter working in Philadelphia and often with VSBA, whom Izenour dubbed "artist and airbrush extraordinaire."

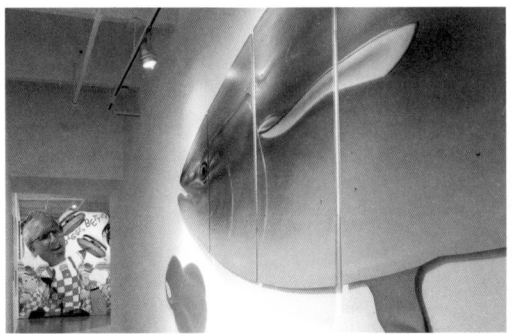

Pages 14–15, opposite, above, and overleaf: Views of the exhibition
"Signs of Fun: The Design Scrapbook of Steven Izenour" at the
FWM, 1995

A-frame

The A-frame was the first structure VSBA built in Maine for Stroud, and was completed in 1998 in association with John Dargis, a highly skilled local builder who would be responsible for all Stroud's construction in Maine, and with Michael Wommack. In the firm's project statement, "A Celebration of the Maine Vernacular—With a Twist," Izenour described the A-frame as a "sign" identifying the A.S.A.P. complex from the road. "The vernacular tradition of ordinary shingle capes, sheds, and barns . . ." he said, "ordinary work-a-day buildings, have been the inspiration for Kamp Kippy . . . But the commercial vernacular of roadside Maine . . . is equally indigenous and valid, a tradition of big lobster signs, A-frames, trailers, lawn ornaments . . ."[4] Izenour combined both vernacular traditions, decorating the simple shingle cladding with a trompe l'oeil painted sky and the deck elevations with painted metal friezes made of lawn ornaments—"pink flamingos and Ma & Pa farmers, whirly-gigs writ large."[5] The friezes were fabricated by Steven Schultz, who would produce all the perforated aluminum art graphics that decorated the A.S.A.P. buildings. Stroud's beloved dog, Forrest Gump, made an appearance as a yellow Labrador lawn ornament, welcoming visitors at the A-frame entrance. "It's a way to personalize by ornamentation," Izenour said in an interview, "the space between . . . homes and the highway."[6] An early, undated sketch of the A-frame is inscribed "<u>A</u>rt with A capital <u>A</u> or <u>A</u>n <u>A</u>-frame For <u>A</u>n <u>A</u>rtist," therein transforming a graphic sign (the letter "A") into a concept for a basic building type. "Kamp Kippy" was spelled out in twigs over the door. Inside the A-frame, Izenour inserted what he described as a "series of vaults" to mask the insistent A-section ("not unlike a Russian stave church").[7] The vaults were inspired by acoustical baffles originally designed by his father, George Izenour, a theater and lighting designer. They reveal the interior to be a beautiful, sculptural space, an effect unexpected from the simple geometrical shape of the exterior. The interior of the A-frame was unfinished in the summer of 1998 when the building opened: its program was still (even to this day) undefined, "more a sculpture than a functional building" Izenour told a reporter from the *Bar Harbor Times*.[8] The back stairs of the A-frame however, were originally meant to be sat on—an amphitheater for outdoor performances, extending the building beyond its walls and engaging the surrounding landscape.

Two paintings from the Neuf Series by the
artist Edgar Heap of Birds at the original
Billings Barn, 1997

In June 1998, Stroud arranged to rent the Brightside Boathouse in Northeast Harbor to celebrate the completion of the A-frame with an exhibition and lecture by Izenour. "The New/ Old Maine Vernacular" opened on August 28, celebrated with cocktails, dinner, and a slide presentation. Izenour decorated the boathouse interior with graphic representations of the A-frame and some of its ornamental elements were airbrushed directly on the wall by Michael Wommack. At almost full scale, the wall graphics gave visitors to the exhibition a sense of Izenour's humor, how the building felt as realized (as opposed to a drawing), and the importance of scale in general to his work.

At the same time, Izenour was providing wall decorations for the FWM in Philadelphia, fabricating three-dimensional objects out of Venturi's Flowers surface pattern, modified in color and scale. Izenour had the flowers laser-cut out of Sintra PVC foam board, painted by Wommack, and applied to the stairwell connecting the fifth and sixth floors of the FWM, their apparently random positions carefully plotted. Again at about the same time, Izenour gave Stroud a miniature A-frame, airbrushed and ornamented, to use as a mailbox, followed shortly thereafter by a mailbox decorated with Flowers. These were just two of a number of small projects Izenour designed for Stroud.

Shore Cottage Renovations

While the A-frame was under construction, VSBA was engaged in the renovation of Shore Cottage as a residence for Stroud and for the pressing communal needs of A.S.A.P. An addition to the cottage was proposed and revised in 1996–97 to address the preparation of meals for A.S.A.P.'s dining and lecture programs, (an entryway and bathroom were added to the old kitchen, a carport project was abandoned) but as work was simultaneously progressing on the Deer Acres complex across Indian Point Road, it became clear that temporary structures could be erected and used more economically until Deer Acres was functional. Stroud applied for and received a permit from the town of Bar Harbor to construct a tubular tent/awning on a wooden deck. The tent was to exist on a deck addition which would match the existing deck of the cottage. The original yellow lecture tent was erected and taken down every summer on the wooden platform inside the

Water and Wind by Mineo Mizuno at the
Billings farm, 1998

William Wegman and Batty, one of his
Weimerauners, at Acadia National Park, 2003

U-shaped wings of the cottage. In 2003 Stroud had a new white tent made and painted in place by Wommack with Izenour's version of the Flowers pattern. There were many discussions about the tents. In April 1999 Izenour wrote Stroud concerning outstanding issues, among them "the tent, lecture hall, temporary kitchen, slides, and P.A. system all of which we discussed, and we need to spend some time on it and order equipment."[9] In July, Izenour addressed the use of the lecture tent: "I realize that the tent is a bit up in the air . . . but since you have a valid permit my guess is that we will be using it for the next couple of summers and therefore we really should build the projection booth . . . I think it's still worth doing and it would certainly help the acoustics in the tent to isolate the projection noise."[10] Accordingly, a temporary slide booth was designed by Izenour and made that summer, a moveable cabinet with an "Ektachrome" facade containing slides and projector equipment, shaped like a little storage shed (or an outhouse), on wheels.

The first temporary cook shack at Shore Cottage was faced with blue translucent, corrugated panels on the walls and roof. It glowed beautifully at night, like a Japanese lantern, but so effectively prevented heat from escaping that temperatures soared. John Dargis was able to retrofit the shack with insulation, cedar siding and roofing to make it easier to keep cool, and eventually replaced it with a permanent commercial-scale auxiliary kitchen. From 1997, Stroud employed VSBA associates in Maine to work on-site on her architectural projects, Lauren Jacobi most consistently, along with Andrew Pasonick. In spring 1999 Izenour wrote Stroud regarding "summer hires: Lauren (Jacobi) is going back up, but I can't give you Steve Van Dyck all summer—I need him here in the office although he is available to spend 50 percent of his time on your projects and is willing to go back and forth during the summer."[11]

Deer Acres Renovations: Farmhouse and Barn

Although the view of Northwest Cove from Shore Cottage was particularly beautiful, the farmhouse and surrounding property across the road at Deer Acres better lent itself to development for A.S.A.P. "It puts the offices, library, meeting room, dinner/lecture room, kitchen, cocktail porch, etc. in one efficient compact location," Izenour rationalized to Stroud. "Proximity to the main road makes access very easy. With sites 1 and 2 we have ample parking

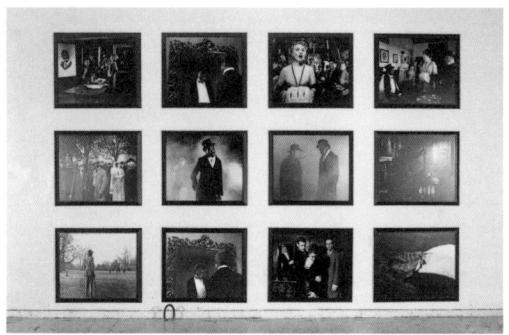
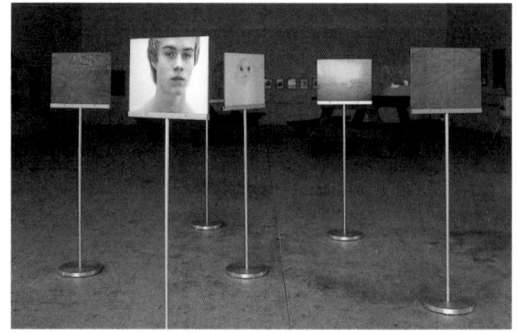

A.S.A.P. exhibition at the Brightside Boathouse, Northeast Harbor,
Maine, displaying Yinka Shonibare's *Dorian Gray* (left) and Roni
Horn's *Doubt by Water* (right), 2004

available. And last but not least . . . it gets the whole operation out of your and Clint's living room."[12] Accordingly, VSBA renovated and extended the old farmhouse to house A.S.A.P. offices, library, meeting rooms, staff apartments, and a full institutional kitchen to prepare meals for the dinner/lecture programs. Additions (still ongoing) "were done in the spirit of extended Maine farmhouses—one gabled box smashing into the next," according to VSBA's project statement.[13] The architects "made a conscious effort to preserve a traditional view from the road with the small windows of a 'cape,'" but were "much freer and graphic with the scale of the openings" on the east facades that both framed entrances to the complex from the driveway and parking area[14] and maximized views of the pond and surrounding trees.

Izenour was VSBA principal-in-charge and project director of the complex at Deer Acres. He designed the farmhouse renovations as well as the T-shirt house and Palette house additions. Work on the farmhouse and its additions began in 1996, the design phase of certain elements of the farmhouse continuing through 1999 and beyond, among them, the kitchen, which Stroud, Izenour, and VSBA architects Claudia Cueto and Tim Kearney studied together in January 1998. Stroud knew what she wanted: wide aisles so that two persons could pass each other comfortably; a lighting scheme that included indirect lighting (requiring VSBA to revise their initial plan); and white cabinets more "Shaker" in their style.[15] The signature VSBA space in the farmhouse was the library on the first floor, with a frieze of "BOOKS" produced in big, three-dimensional letters to stand above the library shelves and "HOME" bracketed by flames on the hearth surround, alternately shown in a drawing and eventually realized with the words "FIREPLACE" and "HEARTH." Like those of the A-frame, the library signs could be read; their words voiced the simple functions of the structures, a consistent, humorous, and particularly apt device in a room designed for reading.

Work on the library, however, was continually deferred. In July 1999 Izenour wrote Stroud: "The library: who does it, when do we do it? I assume since you're probably using the space for temporary office that this is a winter project?"[16] In September he wrote again, "What should we do about library fireplace, i.e., Wommack's 'flames?'"[17] Design issues seem to have been involved because in October he sent new drawings. "Also, as you requested, we took a fresh look at the

Lobster picnic for A.S.A.P. guests on a boat heading to Bakers Island

library: we lowered the books . . . frieze to account for ceiling irregularities. We redid interior with wood bookshelves, desks, etc. as per the original library design."[18] The following spring, Steve van Dyck worked on lighting for the library and in June 2000, Izenour and Stroud discussed the shelves again: "Dear Kippy, I spoke too soon about the library shelves, repainting them is easier said than done and it looks like they are sure to chip."[19] The library remained unfinished at Izenour's death in 2001, the project managed thereafter by Claudia Cueto and Tim Kearney, first as associates of VSBA, and after 2004, as partners in their own firm, CuetoKearney Architects. In 2002 Kearney wrote Stroud: "The BOOKSBOOKSBOOOKS frieze for the library is ready for your review. The fireplace surround and hearth still need to be finalized."[20]

VSBA additionally helped Stroud renovate an old barn near the farmhouse for use as a studio, storage, and drive-through garage. The barn was listed in VSBA's 1999 A.S.A.P. project schedule to design steel and framing and with consultation from Stroud's friend, architect John Lucas, to specify windows and doors. "Enclosed please find the latest drawings of the Deer Acres Barn," Izenour and van Dyck wrote Stroud in May 1999.

> These drawings include all of the elements we discussed this past weekend. We feel very good about these results . . . of particular note is a new window type that we've chosen . . . for John Lucas' elevation. On E-1 you will notice that these windows are now more similar to the existing window on top that we'd like to keep. They are three panes across instead of four, and definitely a more typical barn window. We believe that this is in tune with John Lucas' aesthetics for this elevation. Also, the clearstory windows above the front sliding door now fit within the doorframe as you requested . . . Just to reiterate—we are very pleased with the overall aesthetics of the building's exterior. In our collaboration we feel that we've come up with a building much more in touch with the Maine vernacular.[21]

Deer Acres Additions: T-shirt House and Palette House
Izenour's first drawings for the T-shirt house in 1996 and the Palette house in 1997 show that like

Left: Steve Izenour's presentation board showing examples of Maine architecture, exhibited at "The New/Old Maine Vernacular" at the Brightside Boathouse, June 1998

Above: Steven Izenour, Anthony Bracali, and Michael Wommack (left to right) at "The New/Old Maine Vernacular" exhibition. Overleaf: Aerial view of Stroud's properties on both sides of Indian Point Road, Bar Harbor, Maine, looking toward Northwest Cove

Venturi, he tended to define his visual and theoretical approach early in the design process, and while flexible, rarely waver from it. When the A-frame opened with a lecture/reception at the Brightside Boathouse in the summer of 1998, a flyer announcing the event was decorated with drawings of the three buildings—A-frame, T-shirt, and Palette—all standing like billboards, designed from the outside in. According to VSBA's project statement, the T-shirt and Palette houses were additions

> in the tradition of an extended New England farmhouse . . . added directly onto an older kitchen . . . This addition is a simple barn-like structure . . . A major feature is a large two-story window in the shape of an abstract A.S.A.P. T-shirt with a stainless steel letter frieze [with the words 'Kamp Kippy']. Next to, and inflected to the 'barn' is a new garage/studio building with a garage on the lower level and a studio space above. The painting studio has a large 'palette' window facing the pond to the east. The farmhouse, 'T-shirt,' 'barn,' 'palette house,' and existing barn form an informal, drive-in 'Maine farmyard' introduction to Kamp Kippy.[22]

The complex of farmhouse, T-shirt, Palette, and the most recent addition, the Flower house, is perfectly situated within the surrounding rural context, celebrating and using the vocabulary of traditional Maine architecture. These are quiet buildings, beautifully crafted with shingle siding, wood, and gabled roofs. The difference from local structures comes in the size of the VSBA windows, their shapes and placement on the facades, as well as all of the applied decoration.

The T-shirt house, housing the A.S.A.P. offices and staff apartments, was completed largely in 1999. A punch list, assembled by Izenour and Van Dyck in February, included for VSBA and Stroud: detailing trim conditions, finalizing basement windows, detailing accessories (coat-racks, mailboxes, bulletin boards, etc.), detailing first-floor bathroom graphics and bathroom counter, and detailing exterior decking and stairs.[23] The same list showed that John Dargis was to complete wainscoting, trim, flooring, and deck built-ins, and to paint the interior, install appliances and

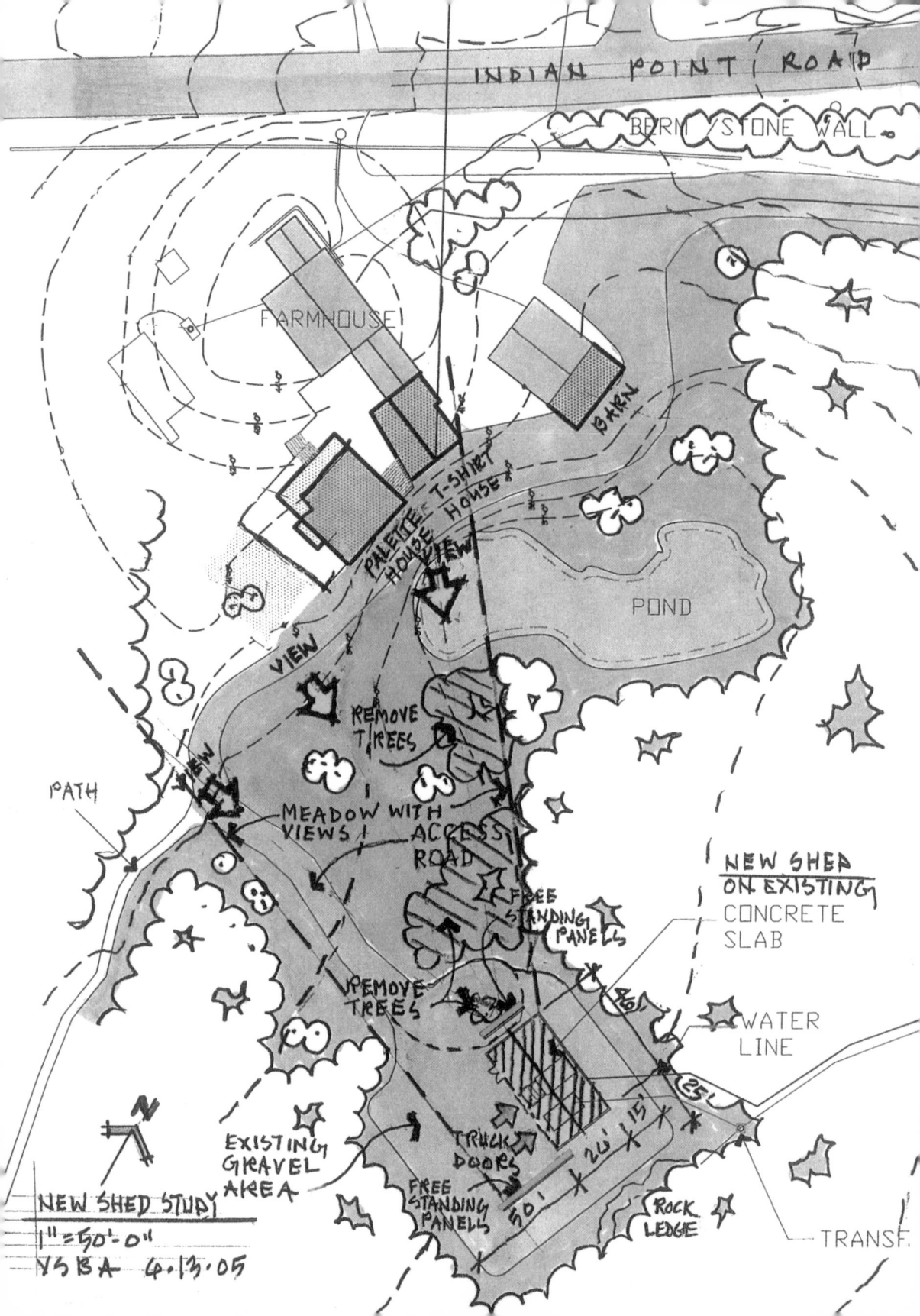

INDIAN POINT ROAD

BERM / STONE WALL

FARMHOUSE

BARN

PALETTE / T-SHIRT HOUSE

HOUSE

VIEW

VIEW

POND

REMOVE TREES

VIEW

MEADOW WITH VIEWS!

ACCESS ROAD

FREE STANDING PANELS

PATH

REMOVE TREES

NEW SHED ON EXISTING CONCRETE SLAB

WATER LINE

N

EXISTING GRAVEL AREA

TRUCK DOORS

FREE STANDING PANELS

50' 20' 15'

ROCK LEDGE

25'

TRANSF.

NEW SHED STUDY
1" = 50'-0"
YSBA 4·13·05

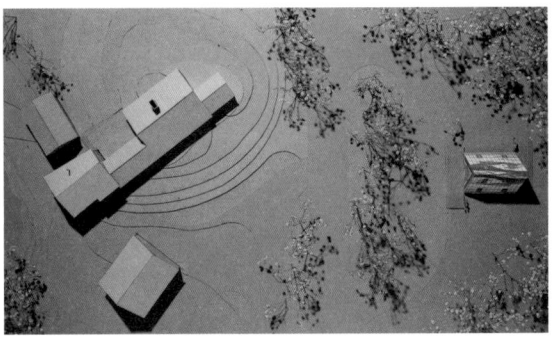

Opposite: "New Shed Study" by VSBA dated June 13, 2005, with schematic plan of the Best Panel garage and sight lines toward the Best Products panels. This hand-drawn plan reveals VSBA's careful attention to views of the garage from various vantage points on the site. Above: Schematic design model of Deer Acres farmhouse and barn by VSBA

fixtures, and the basement windows. Like the farmhouse library, the bathroom on the first floor of the T-shirt was a signature space, painted on walls and ceiling with images of grass, blue sky, fluffy white clouds, and a three-dimensional red lobster floating incongruously over a white picket fence, executed partly in three-dimensions. The basic green, blue, and white palette of the bathroom was very like that of the A-frame, the decoration similarly confounding expectations of indoor/outdoor realities. Steve and Andy Pasonick asked Stroud in September whether she wanted the picket fence and Mike Wommack to airbrush it as in the design rendering; if so, they said, Mike would be willing to come up the first week in October.[24]

Originally conceived as a utility building with studio space (an old generator shed occupied the site and the initial plan was to enlarge it with an apartment above), the Palette house was designed and redesigned largely over a period of some eight years (1997–2005), but continually modified and worked on to the present day as Stroud and Izenour rethought the program, and as the need to create a better facility for A.S.A.P.'s dinners and lectures became more acute. Existing drawings show a multitude of layouts and floor plans for the use of the building, from one or more studios over a carport/garage in 1997, to schemes with and without kitchens and various proposals for dining (tents, screened porches, covered dining) in 1999–2000. In fall 1999 Izenour proposed (but never built) a lighthouse next to the Palette house—a paneled sign structure with a circular stair behind it, the stair ascending to the rooftop of the Palette house where a widow's walk was to be placed for views. Here, too, the artist's palette, which like the T-shirt was originally conceived as a composition of windows (appearing as such on the 1998 Brightside Boathouse flyer), became (and remained) an applied panel on the facade of the building, no longer an integral part of the building, but a surface application. The lighthouse was part of a major redesign campaign to make the Palette house bigger and more versatile, to "work for summer program dinner/lectures," Izenour wrote Stroud,

> . . . we added eight feet on the west (the kitchen deck end) and four feet on the east. This gives us a total of 1,340 square feet and easily sits seventy plus for dinner and ninety plus for lectures . . . We increased the width of the main door

Drawing of elevation of Deer Acres farmhouse and additions proposed
by Steven Izenour in 1999. The Palette house is shown with a lighthouse
and widow's walk. The A-frame, completed in 1998, appears across
Indian Point Road.

> . . . to give a gracious entrance, i.e., cocktails on the deck and proceed up to
> dinner and lectures . . . We left big white walls on the north and south so that
> the room can be used as a studio or exhibit/museum . . . We added a big, circular
> window on the west for the setting sun and the view of the pond, and we removed
> the big window on the east to give us a third large white wall for projection/
> gallery/studio. We added a projection/lighting balcony on the west end to get
> the cameras off the floor and out of the way . . . We think this is a damn good
> building, meets the program and makes for a real nice contained Arcadia [sic]
> complex. We hope you like it.[25]

Stroud must have had reservations about the dining/lecture space in addition to questions about the deed restrictions on the property[26] because Izenour wrote her the following month concerning new schemes A and A[1] and B: "Dear Kippy, I hope all of the pain is worth it! Based on our discussion last Friday and a long discussion with Lauren, as you suggested. Here is what we came up with to try to make the Palette, Farmhouse complex work as the A.S.A.P. headquarters next year."[27] Izenour tenaciously tried to resolve the design issues and move the project forward: "If we sign off on the Palette House between now and Christmas, we can have drawings done in January and up to Dargis. So with any luck, since this is a one-room building, we could have it up and running by June."[28] Stroud, however, was not ready to sign off and redesign occupied most of 2000. By June, the two had agreed only on the need for a bigger building that would involve expanding the foundation (already poured). The basic question concerned Palette house's ability to accommodate both dining and lecture functions, which typically had been separated at Shore Cottage. "I thought your idea of a dining deck was brilliant and solves a lot of problems," Izenour wrote to Stroud, "close to kitchen, no clean-up problems, close to lectures in Palette."[29] Conceived that summer as a temporary tent (which Izenour proposed having "different artists decorate. . . each season"[30]) or semi-permanent porch, by January 2001, the dining porch had been transformed by Izenour into a "dining barn" plus kitchen because of space issues.[31] "It seems to us that it would make a whole lot more sense than squeezing it into Palette and the porch, where

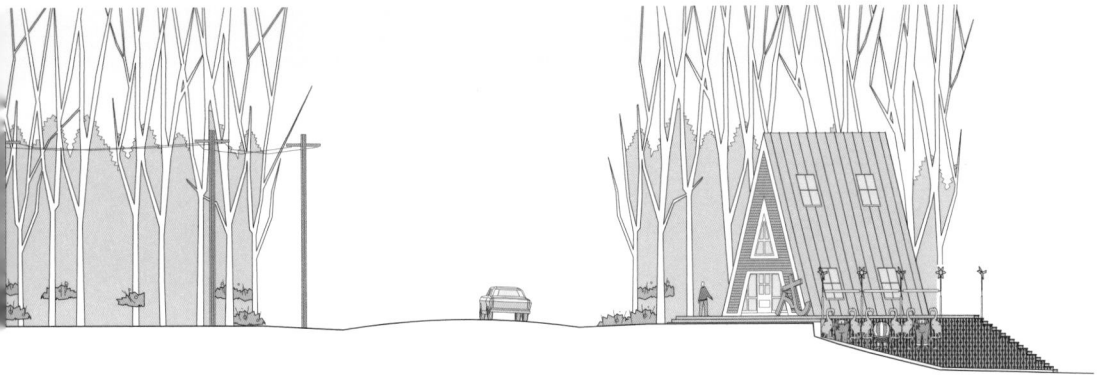

as you so rightly pointed out there is not enough space to do it right."[32] The program was still unresolved in August 2001 when Izenour died unexpectedly. Kearney and Cueto took over the project for VSBA, redesigning the building to make it as large as it could be on the site, and as Stroud agreed, limiting its program to a lecture space adjusted to accommodate new video/recording/projection requirements, with a storage area above. The building was ready for use in 2005 and the palette ornament was completed in October of that year, its beautifully contextual camouflage pattern adapted from VSBA's Penguin Pool design at the New Jersey State Aquarium (1997–98). Kearney had been careful about the placement of the palette. "The palette wants to float on top of the wall. So the pin mounting and the shingling will have to be thought through. Also, the brushes and paint tube will appear to go through the roof eave, sort of the equivalent of the rubber arrow through the head trick."[33]

Temple Shed

In September 2000, Izenour reminded Venturi that Stroud had offered to build "a little Bob house" in Maine. Venturi's first idea was to realize the unbuilt vacation house he had designed in 1967–68 for the Yale architectural historian George Hersey, its facade composed of a circle inscribed in a square. However, as Izenour explained to Stroud:

> Rather than do the Hersey House, which will have real problems with the flat roof, etc. in Maine, he would like to do one of his prototypical 'kid's image of a house' bungalow. It would have basically one room downstairs and two bedrooms upstairs. With your O.K., he would like to go ahead and do some basic drawings for this such as when I come up at the end of the month I could bring them and we could zero in on a site. He said to tell you that he loves you and he has been dying to do this house for twenty-five years . . . The idea is quite simple as you can see from the sketch the house is kind of a kid's symbolic image of a house, door window, pitched-roof and chimney, but it's all done at one-and-a-half normal scale, so while it's small in actual size (20′ x 40′) it is monumental in scale.[34]

Drawings by VSBA of elevations of barn/studios 1 and 2 (unbuilt). The windows
gave the symmetrical and traditional buildings a contemporary update.

Drawing by VSBA of elevations of Robert Venturi's "Little Big"
house (unbuilt)

The last drawing Izenour sent to Stroud in August 2001 was not Venturi's "little house" or another unbuilt residential project, but a simple storage shed with double barn doors at the rear, and a classical temple front taken from Venturi's whimsical 1977 Eclectic House series of interchangeable historical architectural styles. Built on the site of an old well-head house northeast of the farmhouse, the Temple stood at the end of a tree-lined road, a processional approach that mimicked the approach to two other temples well-known to Venturi, the Parthenon in Greece and the Philadelphia Museum of Art (PMA) enthroned at the end of the Benjamin Franklin Parkway. "Here's the 'final' drawings for the well-house/shed," Izenour wrote. "We've increased the size of the door so a pickup can back in, and we've lengthened the building to make it bigger. I'm not showing the aluminum cutout 'PMA facade' on this drawing, since I don't want to make any trouble with code people and this feature is 'temporary' and removable for the winter months. We think this use of removable ornamental devices is a real effective way of having our cake and eating it too; it's cost effective and doesn't take long to slap them back on each season."[35]

Venturi's decorated temple front is simply that—a thin facade for the shed that stands behind it, a signboard, unrelated to the function of the building. There is an interstitial space between the actual shed and the temple front where, passing through, one realizes what is going on behind the artifice—the "decorated shed," a typology invented and expounded in the essays that make up Venturi, Scott Brown, and Izenour's *Learning from Las Vegas* of 1972. As in the "kid's image of a house" Venturi earlier proposed, the proportions of the classic Doric order of the Temple have been altered and exaggerated for monumental effect, with bloated columns, elongated pediment, and oversized ornamental frieze. The following June 2002, Kearney wrote Stroud regarding the building: "Drawings are with John Dargis and we understand that the foundations have been poured (including the piping for radiant heat and plumbing for a sink). The aluminum billboard has been painted and is in Mike Wommack's studio awaiting transport to Maine. John is hopeful that he can get enough of the frame in place to support the temple by Bob and Denise's July visit."[36]

When Izenour died in August 2001, he was remembered by the *New York Times* as

> a principal and leading spirit in the architectural firm of Venturi, Scott Brown and Associates, where he worked for more than three decades. In addition to carrying out his own architectural projects, including the Philadelphia Children's Zoo of 1985 and most recently the new Children's Garden in Camden, New Jersey, Mr. Izenour presided over his firm's exhibition and graphic designs, project presentations, research and office organization . . . [he] organized the trip to Las Vegas and photographed the hotel strips as neon showstoppers and emblems of design's raw potential. He eventually helped write "Learning from Las Vegas" . . . This manifesto on spontaneity as a vital design force has influenced students of architecture and popular culture ever since.[37]

With the help of his colleagues at VSBA, Stroud organized a "Steve Izenour Tribute" exhibition in December 2001 at the FWM. As in "Signs of Fun," the gallery was transformed into an airbrushed landscape by Michael Wommack, the columns now fluorescent pink palm trees with green leafy fronds brushing the ceiling. There were signs everywhere, among them:

"Make no mistake, he'd never admit it, For VSBA, Steve was always a free spirit. Steve's Way is the Highway;" and "With Bob and Denise, Steve found a niche, To celebrate life from high art to kitsch. Steve's Way is the Highway." According to John Izenour: "Tim Kearney, Lauren Jacobi, Mike Wommack, myself and others put the memorial exhibit together. I am so sorry he didn't get to see it, he would have loved it!"[38]

In July 2002, Venturi and Scott Brown came to Maine to review the buildings—particularly the Temple—and participate in A.S.A.P.'s program, both giving illustrated lectures. Venturi began his lecture by saying:

> We haven't been here to see this institution or this program . . . and our job this weekend . . . is to be introduced to this community, especially the architecture and the layout, the planning situation. The main job we have now is to possibly advise and direct and help the organization and Kippy as it evolves . . . The most fascinating thing to me is that this is a unified. . . institutional programmatic entity. But at the same time, it isn't in one place. It is all over the place. It grows very pragmatically . . . A.S.A.P.—maybe the 'P' should stand for Pragmatism. It is fascinating that it has identity and yet in another way—and that is kind of the beauty of it—that it is spread out apart. People can separate and focus a lot of the time and then they come together as a community at other times. I think that is something that is very beautiful and should be encouraged as the community evolves and grows.[39]

Scott Brown must have reviewed the planning needs of A.S.A.P. on the same visit, because a month later, the firm proposed "preparing a digital map of Mt. Desert Island that documents current A.S.A.P. properties and activities and can help us to understand relationships that link them."[40]

Best Panel Garage

In 2005, the porcelain-enameled steel facade panels of the Best Products Company showroom in Langhorne, Pennsylvania, decorated with the Flowers pattern, were removed from the building after the showroom had been sold and scheduled for renovation. VSBA and the new owners gave the panels, which were in largely good condition, to various museums in small groupings, including the Philadelphia Museum of Art. The largest group of forty-eight panels was given to Stroud for use at A.S.A.P. and a "New Shed Study," hand-drawn in June, shows the flower-paneled screens carefully arranged on the site plan to optimize the view of the panels from the other buildings at Deer Acres. By August, VSBA had produced final design drawings. The two-story, 1,200-square-foot garage was designed ostensibly to house maintenance vehicles in the off-season and an artist's studio in the summer, but more importantly, the building provided an excuse to display the panels. In October 2005, VSBA's David Marohn confirmed a verbal agreement with Stroud about the garage that Dargis would build, scheduling completion in spring 2006.[41] Later that month, he wrote to select paint color for the western red cedar siding that clad the building. Like the Temple, the Best panels form a screen wall, an obvious billboard, decorating a shed. According to VSBA's project statement, written in 2005: "To make

Steven Izenour's slide booth with "Ektachrome" facade for
Shore Cottage lecture tent

the building sassy and iconic, the traditional structure (evoking local red-paneled barns) will be flanked front and rear by porcelain enamel panels . . . The free-standing panels feature large, abstract red and white flowers in a 'wallpaper' pattern. Their impressive scale and bright colors bring big life to this little garage."[42]

Deer Acres Additions: Flower House
The idea of creating a separate dining barn next to the Palette house re-emerged sometime around 2005. Although the interior space of the Palette house was complete, the facade away from the T-shirt was never sided, waiting for whatever was to come. As of this writing, the Flower house, named for its applied Flowers decoration, is just underway, intended to accommodate a dining facility on the ground floor, with a handsome gallery space above. In association with Venturi and Scott Brown, Ronald Evitts, formerly a VSBA associate and since 2000, principal of his own firm, Ronald Evitts Architect, assisted in the design of Flower house, its style deferring to other buildings in the Deer Acres complex. A green flowered tent, painted by Michael Wommack, occupied the construction site in the summer of 2008. Still unbuilt is Venturi's Little Big house, listed as "pending" in June 2002. Basic design drawings were completed that year, "with further massaging . . . (to be) done when a site is located."[43] That is yet to come, along with a media center, still a gleam in Stroud's eye.

Notes

1. Meeting minutes: Robert Venturi, Marion Boulton Stroud, John Izenour, Kathryn B. Hiesinger, and Kathryn E. Higgins, September 22, 2009, Department of European Decorative Arts after 1700, Philadelphia Museum of Art, files.

2. Robert Venturi to Marion Boulton Stroud, letter, July 8, 2002, Venturi, Scott Brown and Associates (VSBA) Archives.

3. Robert Venturi, Denise Scott Brown, and Steven Izenour, *Learning from Las Vegas*, Cambridge and London, 1972, p. 8, with thanks to Kathryn E. Higgins for pointing out this reference to the "new landscape."

4. Steven Izenour, Project Statement, "Kamp Kippy—Acadia Summer Arts Program: A Celebration of the Everyday Maine Vernacular—With a Twist," VSBA Archives, undated (1998).

5. Ibid.

6. Nan Lincoln, "A is for Art," *Bar Harbor Times*, September 10, 1998, D1.

7. Steven Izenour, Project Statement, "Kamp Kippy," op. cit.

8. Nan Lincoln, "A is for Art," op. cit.

9. "Two Steves" (Izenour and Van Dyck) to Stroud, Memorandum, April 28, 1999, VSBA Archives.

10. Izenour to Stroud, Memorandum, July 27, 1999, VSBA Archives.

11. "Two Steves," Memorandum, op. cit.

12. Izenour to Stroud, Memorandum, November 30, 1999, VSBA Archives.

13. Steven Izenour, Project Statement, "Kamp Kippy – Acadia Summer Arts Program" op. cit.

14. Ibid.

15. Anthony Bracali to Claudia Cueto, Tim Kearney, Steven Izenour, D. Singer, Memorandum, January 13, 1998, VSBA Archives.

16. Izenour to Stroud, Facsimile, July 27, 1999, VSBA Archives.

17. Izenour to Stroud, Memorandum, September 8, 1999, VSBA Archives.

18. Izenour to Stroud, Memorandum, October 19, 1999, VSBA Archives.

19. Izenour to Stroud, Memorandum, June 9, 2000, VSBA Archives.

20. Tim Kearney to Stroud, Letter, June 4, 2002, VSBA Archives.

21. Izenour and Van Dyck to Stroud, Transmittal Record, May 11, 1999, VSBA Archives.

22. "Kamp Kippy—Acadia Summer Arts Program: A Celebration of the Everyday Maine Vernacular—With a Twist," op. cit.

23. Izenour and Van Dyck to Stroud, Memorandum, February 10, 1999, VSBA Archives.

24. Izenour and Pasonick to Stroud, Memorandum, September 14, 1999, VSBA Archives.

25. Izenour to Stroud, Memorandum, October 19, 1999, VSBA Archives.

26. Izenour had given Stroud his "non-lawyerly interpretation" of the deed earlier in the fall. Izenour to Stroud, Memorandum, September 8, 1999, VSBA Archives.

27. Izenour to Stroud, Memorandum, November 9, 1999, VSBA Archives.

28. Izenour to Stroud, Memorandum, November 30, 1999, VSBA Archives.

29. Izenour to Stroud, Facsimile, August 9, 2000, VSBA Archives.

30. Izenour to Stroud and Kearney, Facsimile, undated, VSBA Archives.

31. Mark Kocent for Tim Kearney to Stroud, Facsimile, January 23, 2001, VSBA Archives.

32. Izenour to Stroud, Facsimile, undated, [c. January 23, 2001], VSBA Archives.

33. Kearney to Steven Schultz, E-mail, February 15, 2005.

34. Izenour to Stroud, Facsimile, September 7, 2000, VSBA Archives.

35. Izenour to Stroud and Dargis, Transmittal Record, [August 14, 2001], VSBA Archives.

36. Kearney to Stroud, Letter, June 4, 2002, VSBA Archives.

37. Julie V. Iovine, "Steven Izenour, 61, Architect of American Pop," *The New York Times*, August 26, 2001, p. 38.

38. John Izenour to Kathryn Hiesinger, E-Mail, January 15, 2010.

39. Robert Venturi, Lecture, July 13, 2002, DVD, Acadia Summer Arts Program.

40. Venturi to Stroud, Letter, August 6, 2002, VSBA Archives.

41. David Marohn to Stroud, Letter, October 4, 2005, VSBA Archives.

42. Venturi, Scott Brown and Associates, Project Statement, "Kamp Kippy" Acadia Summer Arts Program: Best Products Panels Garage, undated (2005), VSBA Archives.

43. Kearney to Stroud, Letter, June 4, 2002, VSBA Archives.

A-FRAME

Page 41: A-frame mailbox by Steven Izenour, with painted decoration
by Michael Wommack. The mailbox demonstrates Izenour's ability to
manipulate the scale of a design to accommodate different programs and
client needs. Pages 42–43: Aerial view of Indian Point Road with Deer
Acres complex at left and A-frame at right. Opposite: Elevation sketch of
A-frame by Steven Izenour, c. 1995

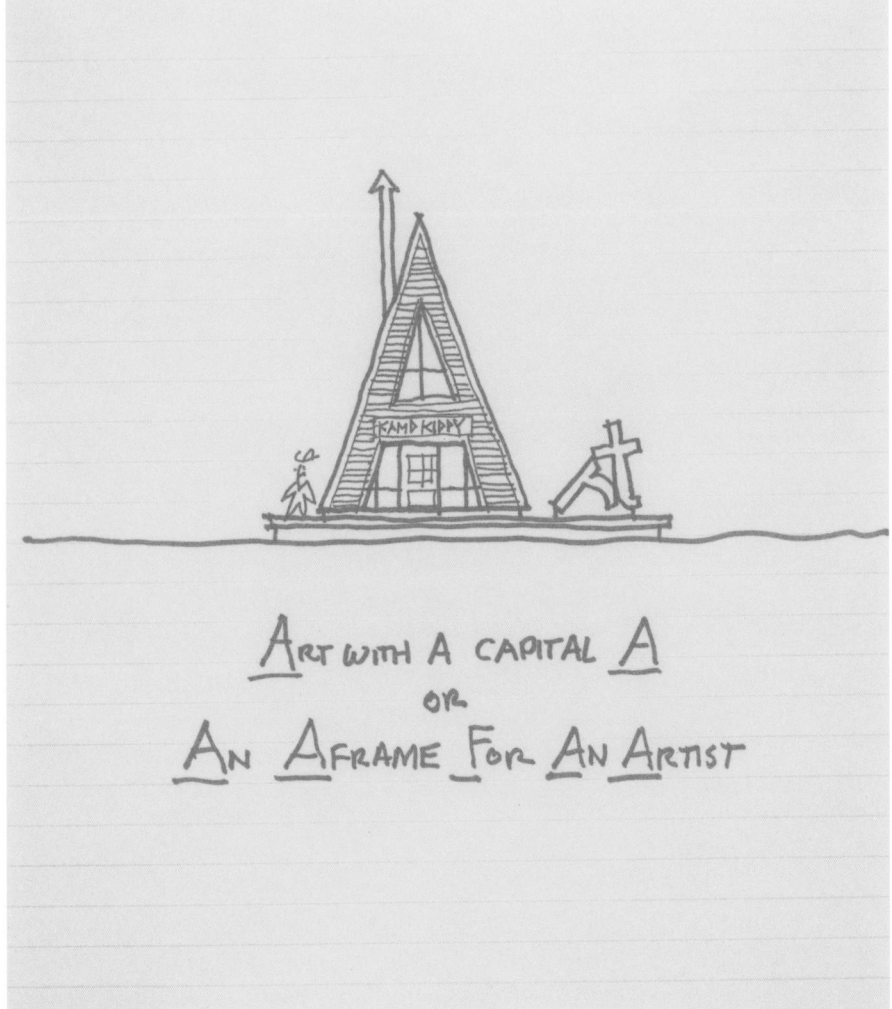

Art with a capital A
or
An Aframe For An Artist

6/2

Drawing of front elevation of A-frame by VSBA

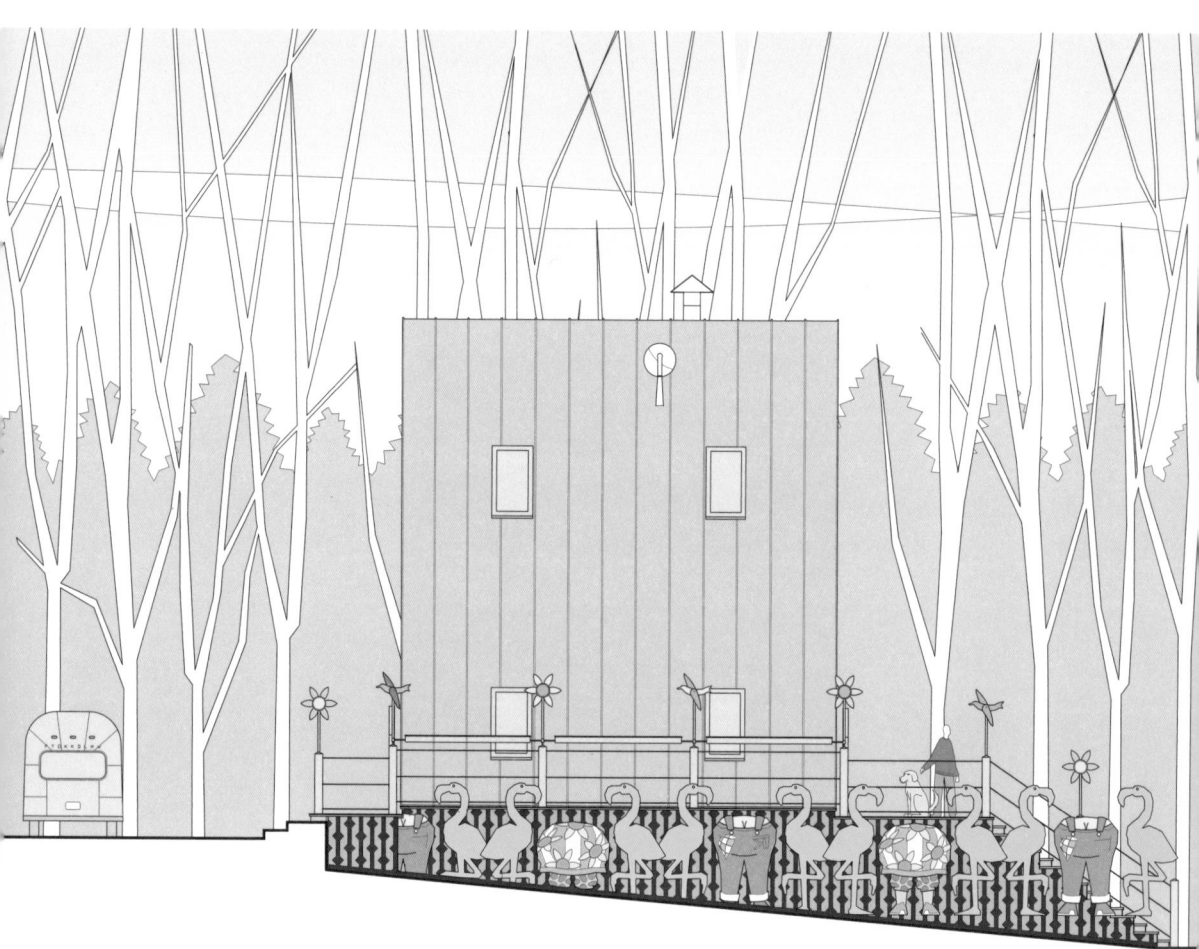

Drawings of side and rear elevations of A-frame by VSBA

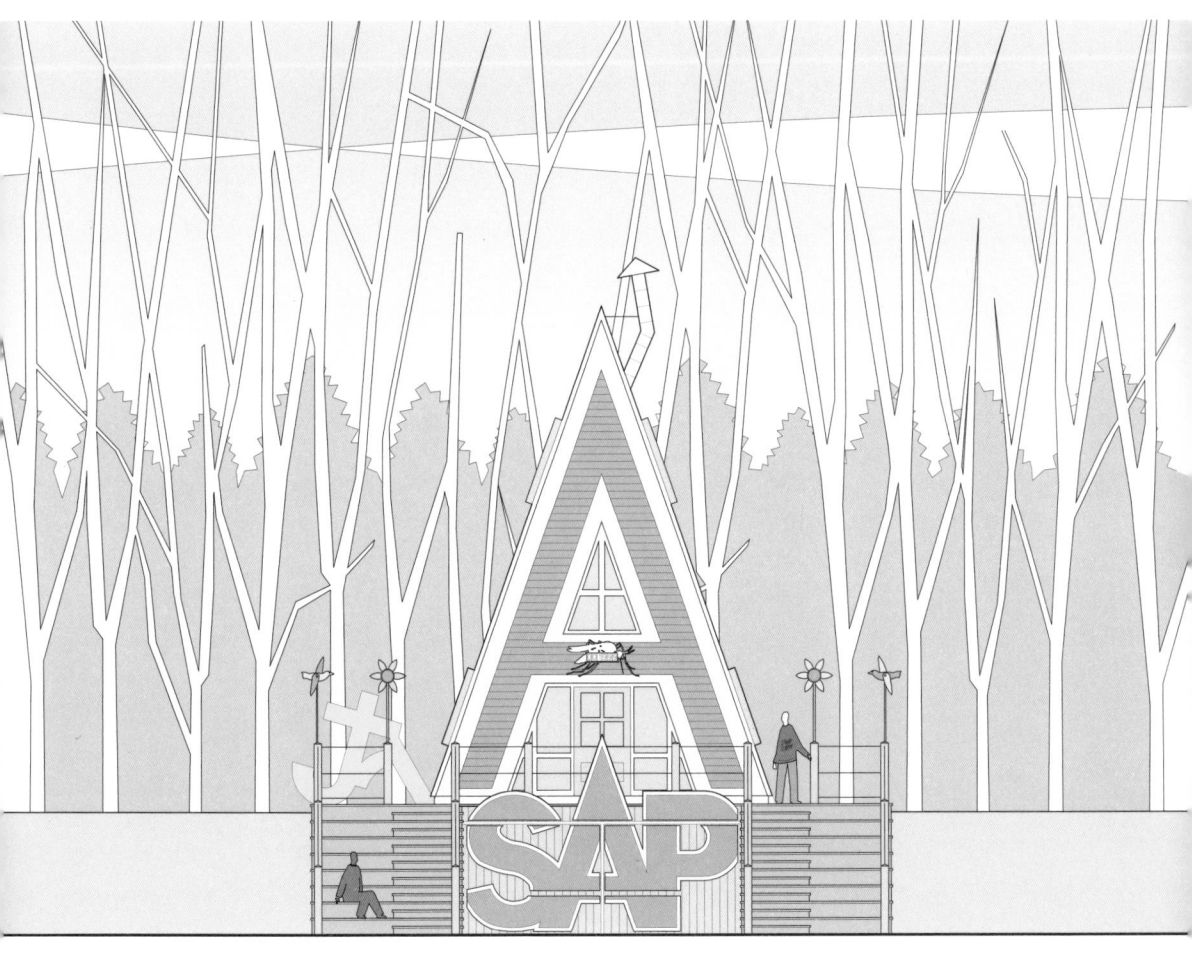

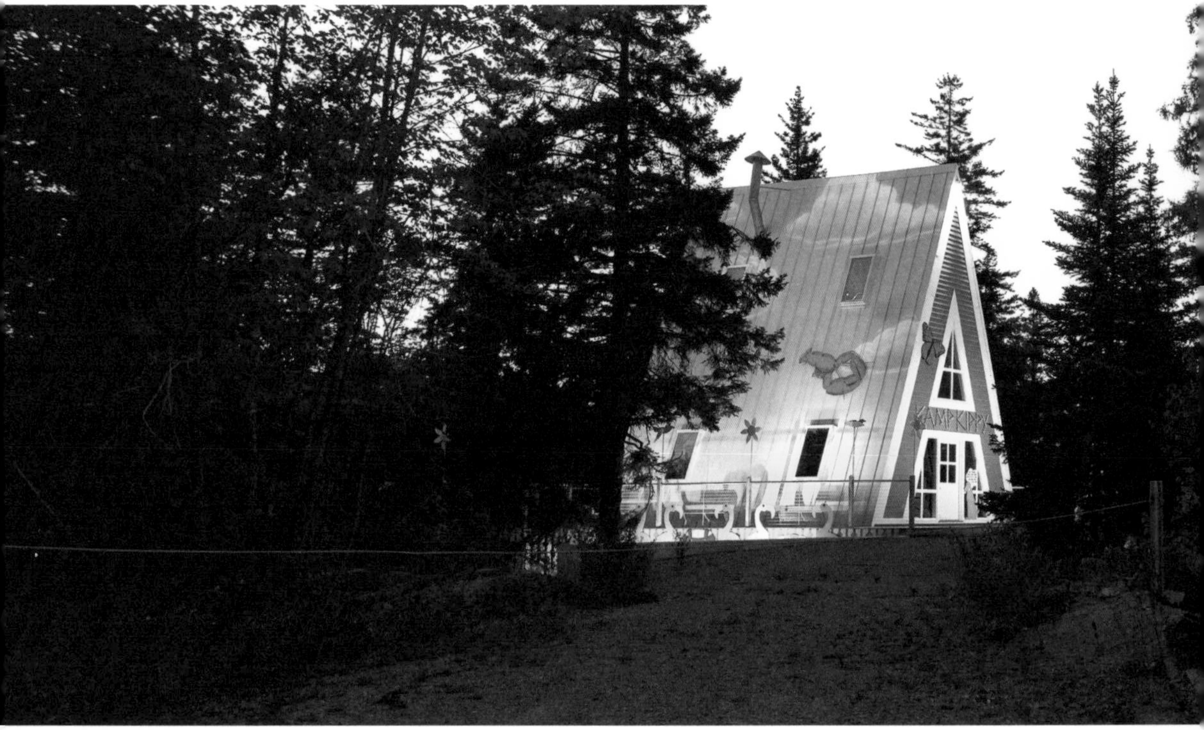

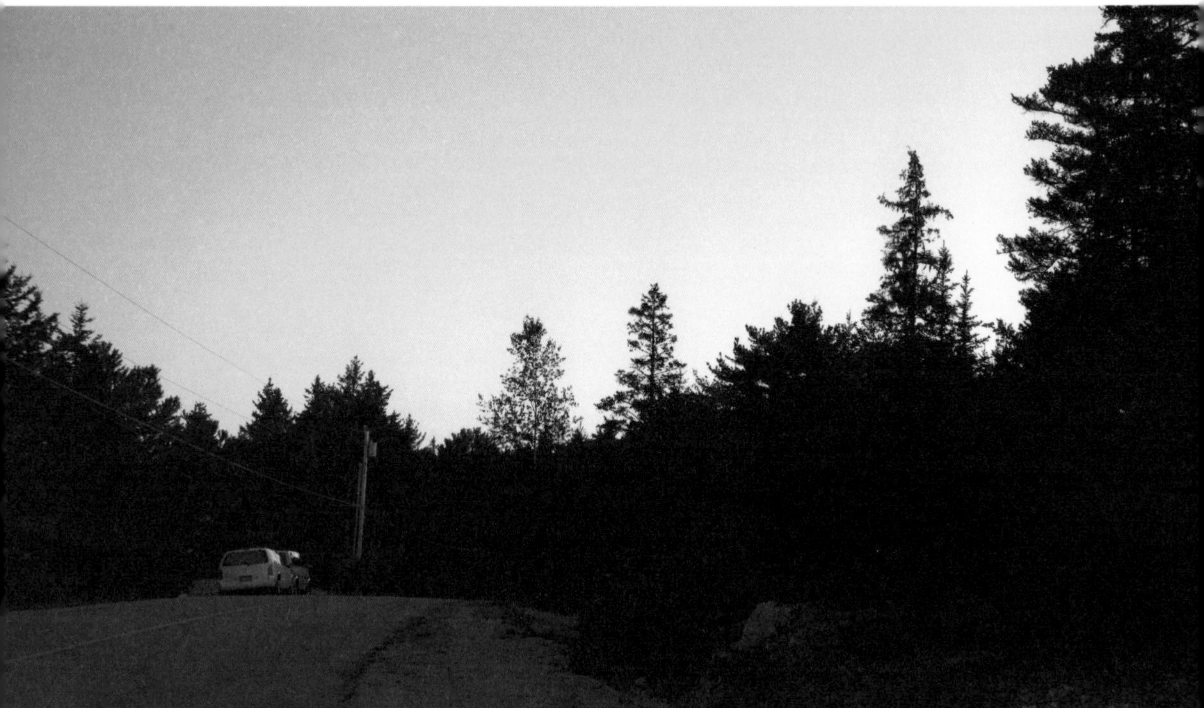

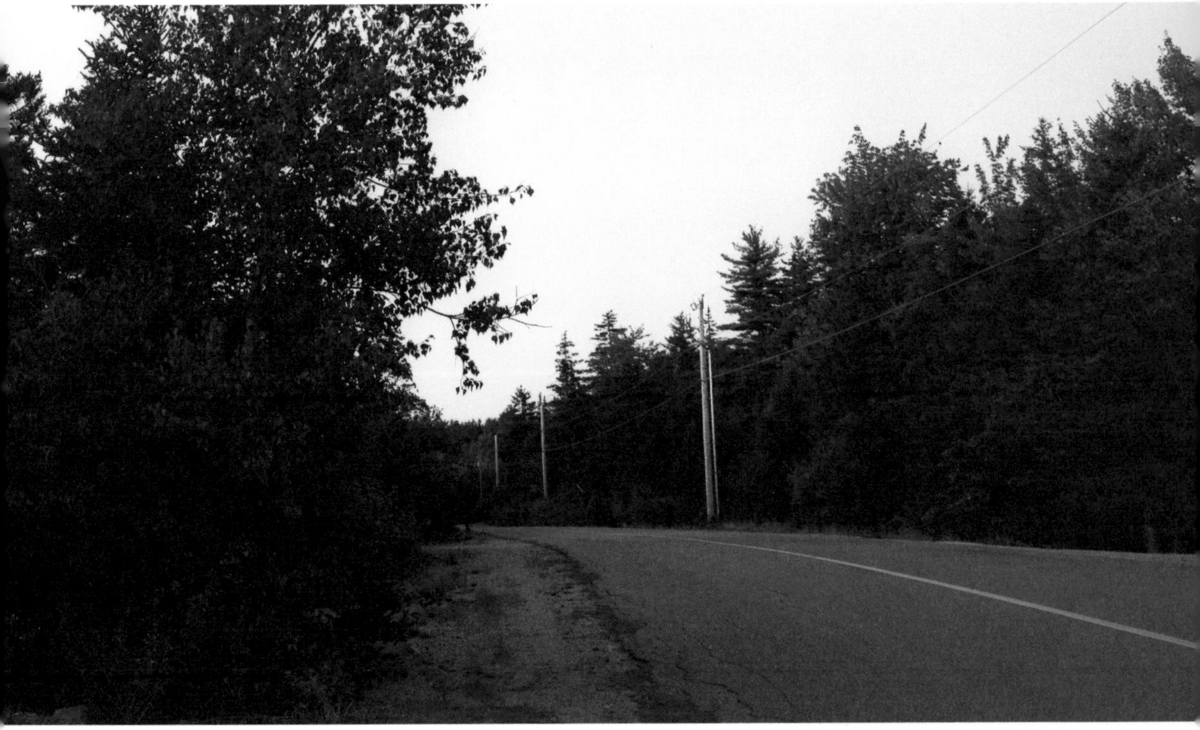

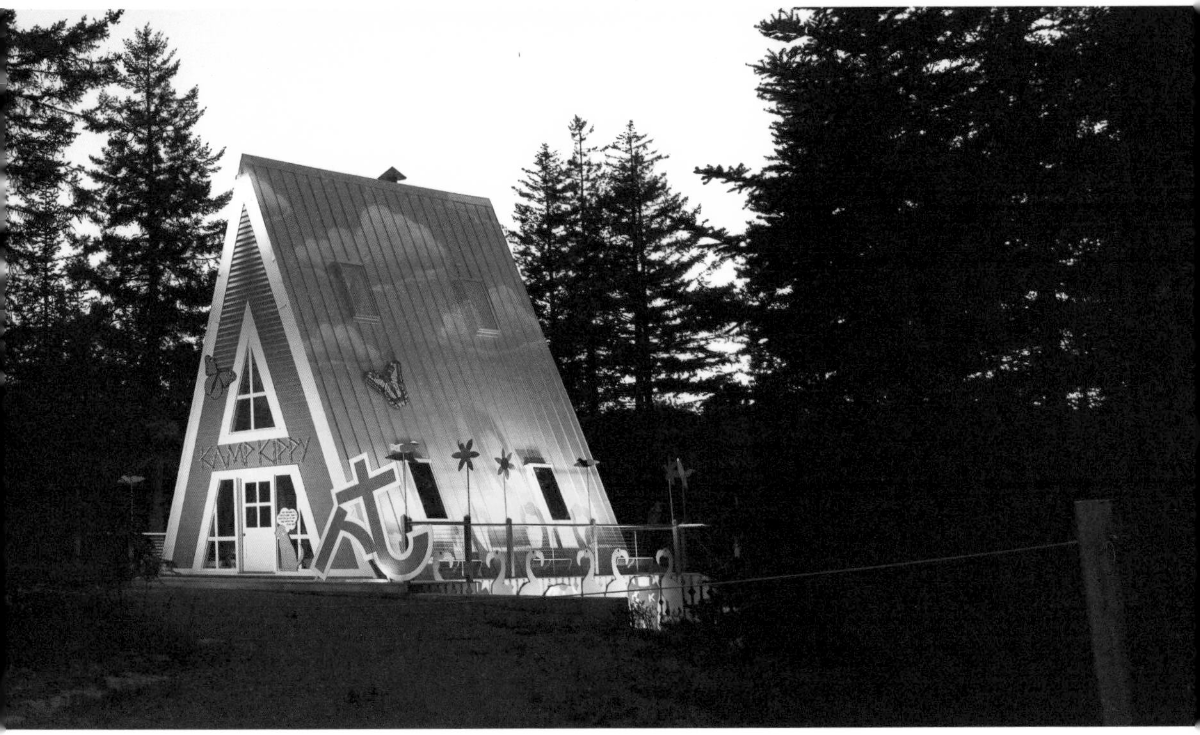
KAMP KIPPY

Forrest Gump A-frame lawn ornament by Steven Izenour,
Michael Wommack, and Steven Schultz. The whirligig was
also proposed for the unbuilt Shore Cottage garage.

Drawing of elevation of A-frame lawn ornaments by Steven
Izenour. Overleaf: A-frame whirligigs and lawn ornaments by
Steven Izenour, Michael Wommack, and Steven Schultz

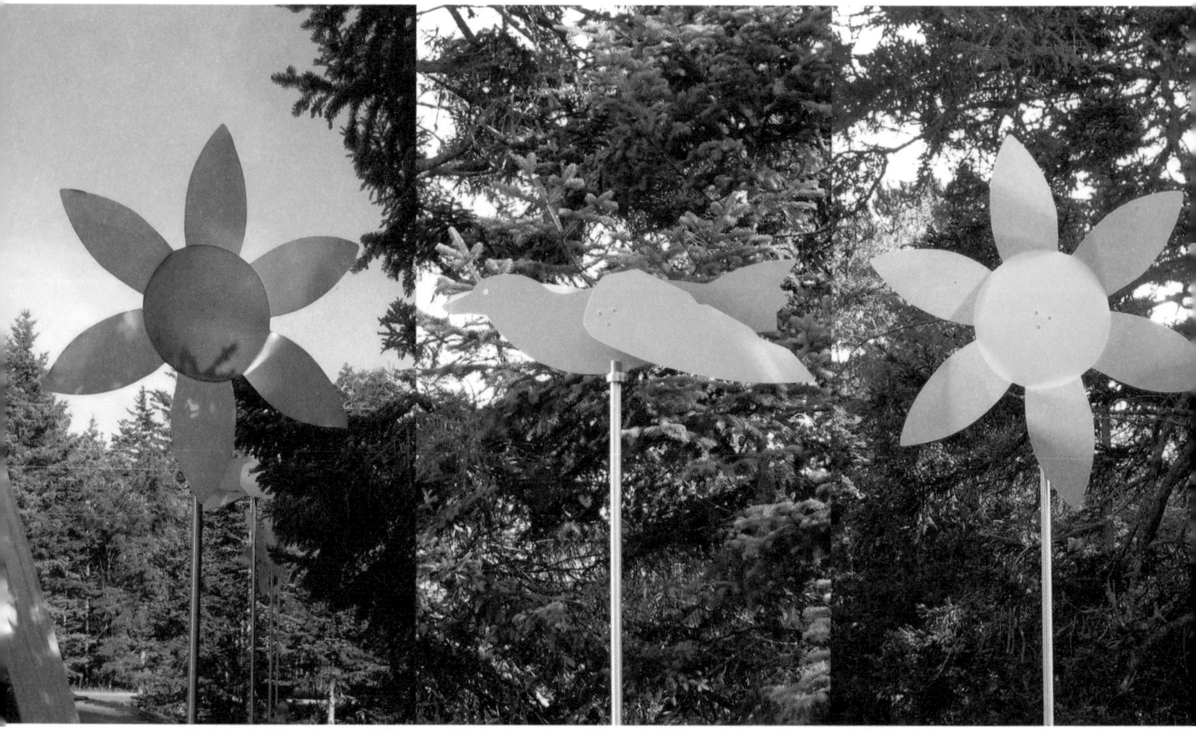

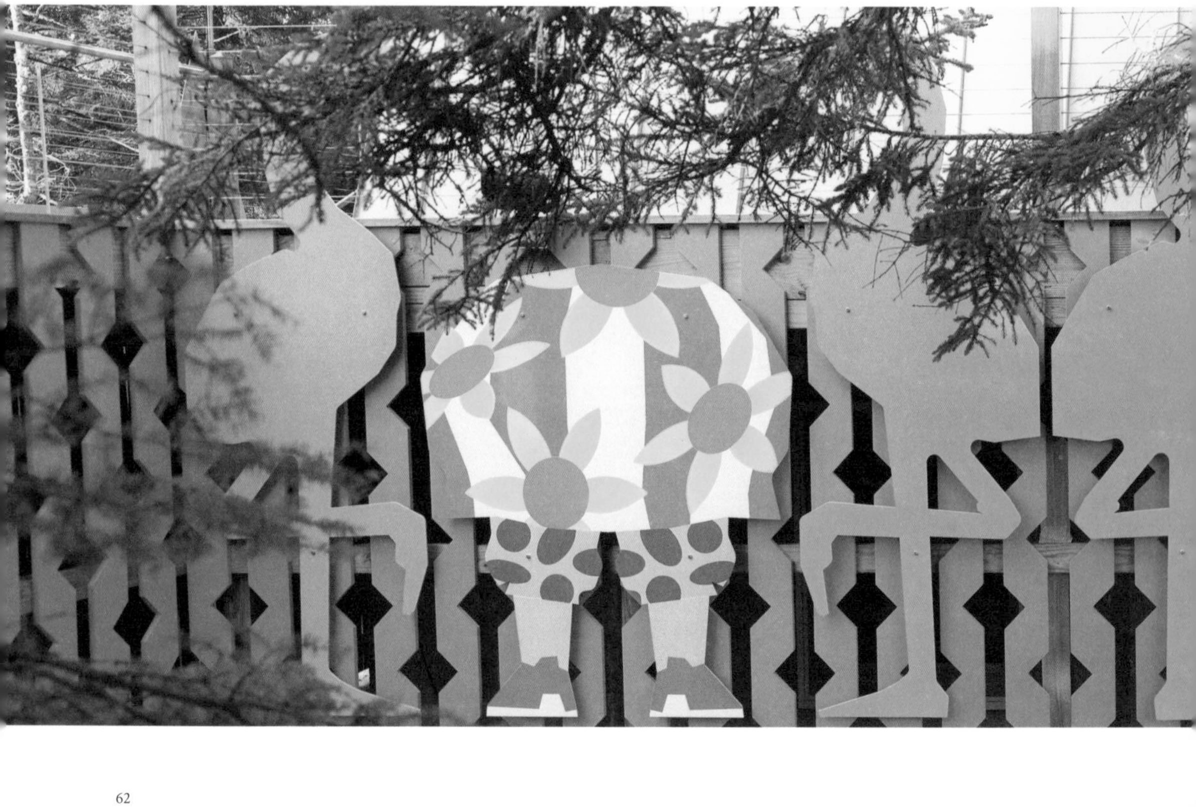

A-frame roof

Two views of the approach to the A-frame entrance (rear facade) from Shore
Cottage. The stairs form an amphitheater for outdoor performances.

"Millennium Bug Zapper" ornament applied to the rear of the A-frame.
Opposite: A-frame interior with "vaults"

SHORE COTTAGE

Page 71: Flowers mailbox by Steven Izenour, with painted decoration by Michael Wommack. Pages 72–73: Aerial view of Shore Cottage. Pages 74–75: Flowers pattern variant by Steven Izenour for the Fabric Workshop and Museum and A.S.A.P. This page: Shore Cottage with Flowers tent for A.S.A.P. dining and lectures, painted by Michael Wommack, 2003

Interior of the Shore Cottage Flowers tent, readied for dining and
illustrated lectures

DEER ACRES

Page 81: Palette and Temple mailboxes by VSBA with painted decoration by Michael Wommack. Pages 82–83: Aerial view of Billings farm. Above: Drawing by VSBA of front elevation of Deer Acres additions, with Temple shed at left, completed 2002

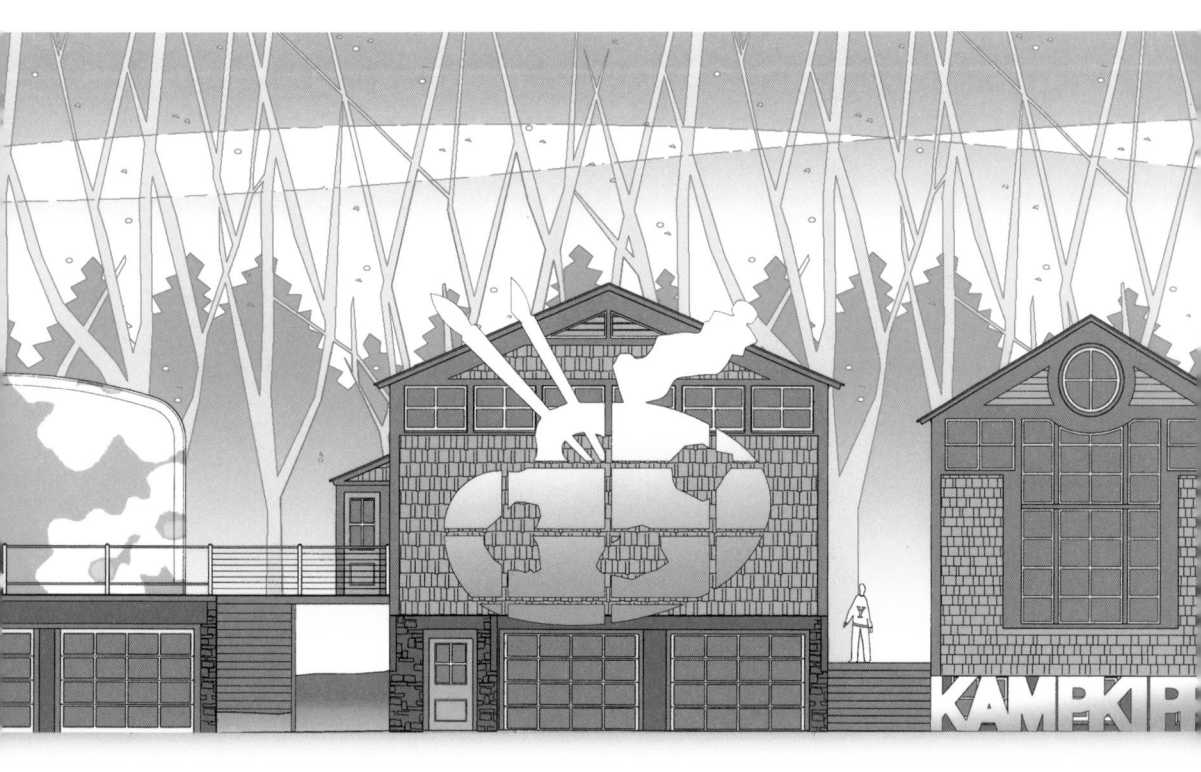

Opposite: T-shirt house at Deer Acres. Overleaf: Flowers tent, Palette
house, and T-shirt house at Deer Acres, 2008

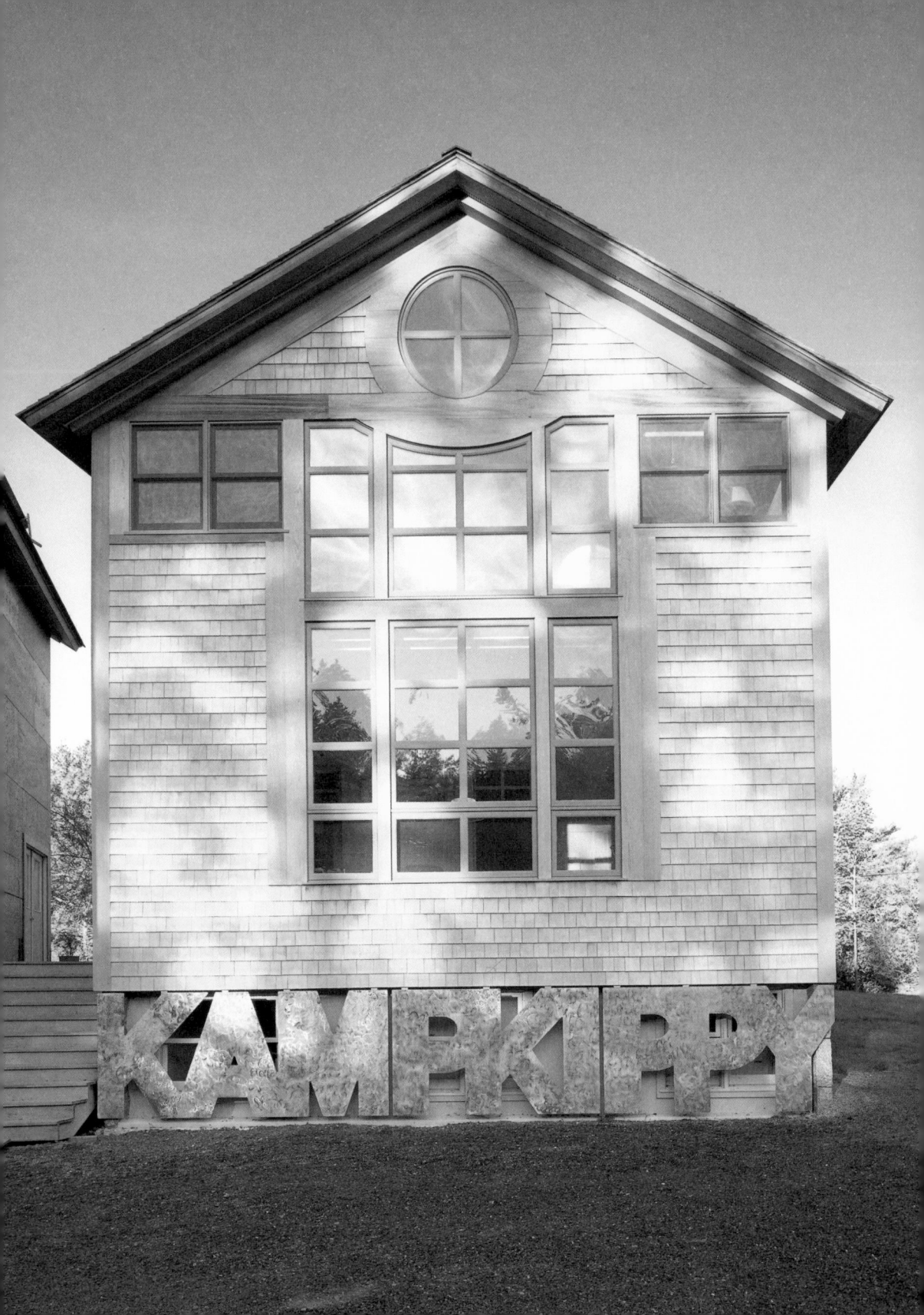

Above and opposite: Two views of Flowers tent. Overleaf: Flower
house (as proposed), with T-shirt house, and Palette house at
Deer Acres

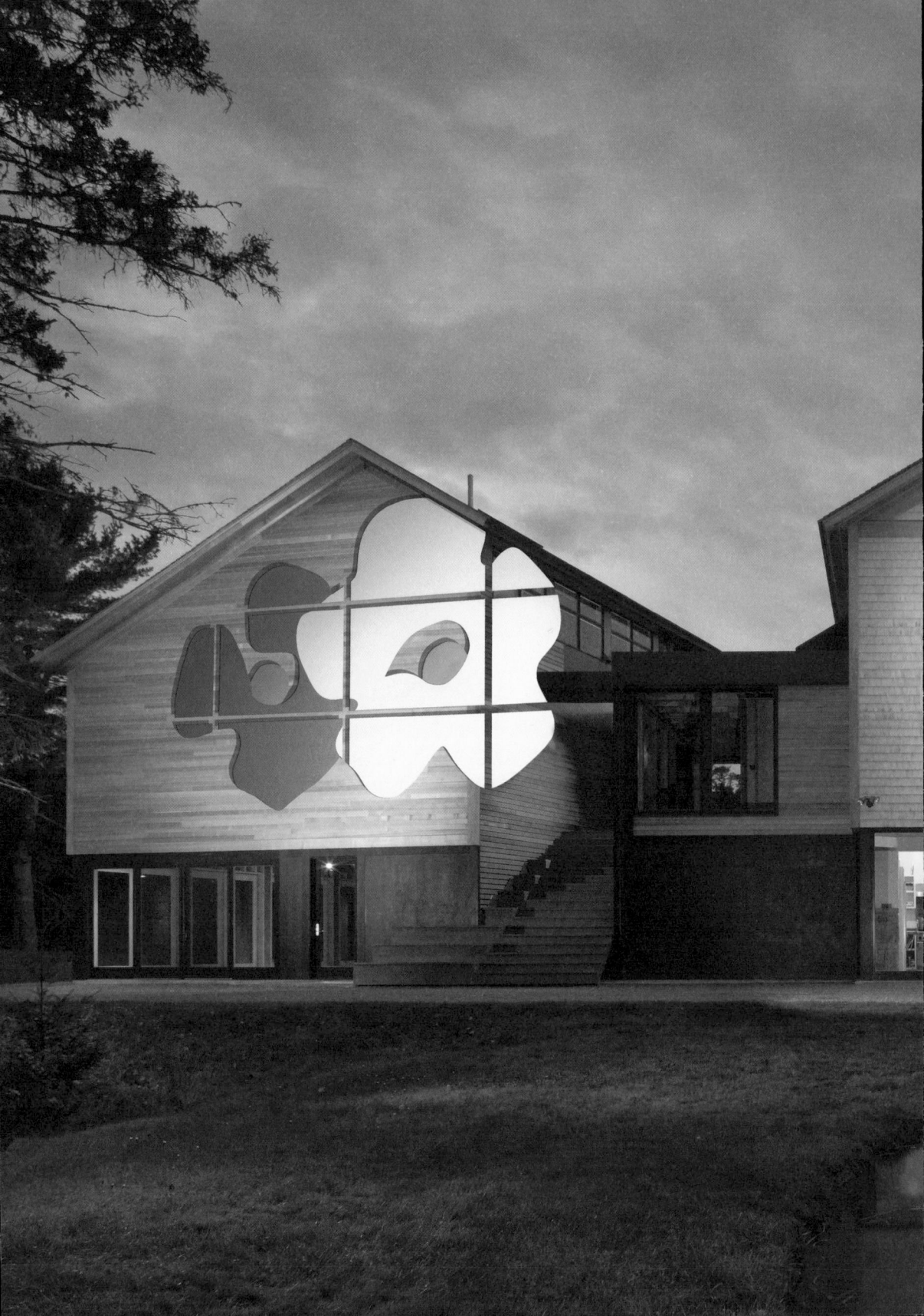

Palette house with applied palette ornament. The camouflage colors
deliberately blend into the surrounding landscape.

View of original Billings farmhouse

Deer Acres complex facing Cadillac Mountain

Opposite: T-shirt house bathroom by Steven Izenour and Michael
Wommack. Overleaf: T-shirt house bathroom detail, lobster wall appliqué

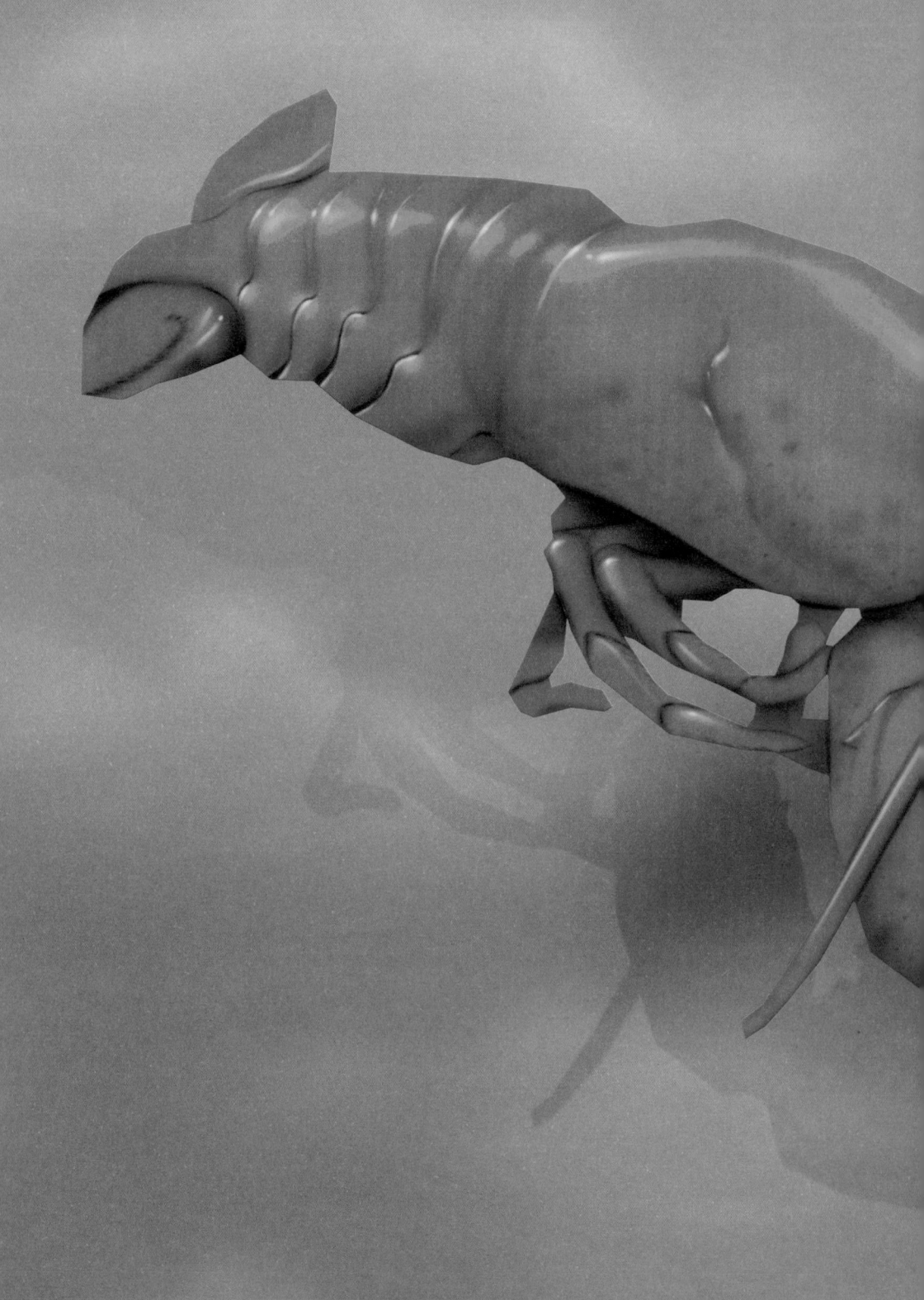

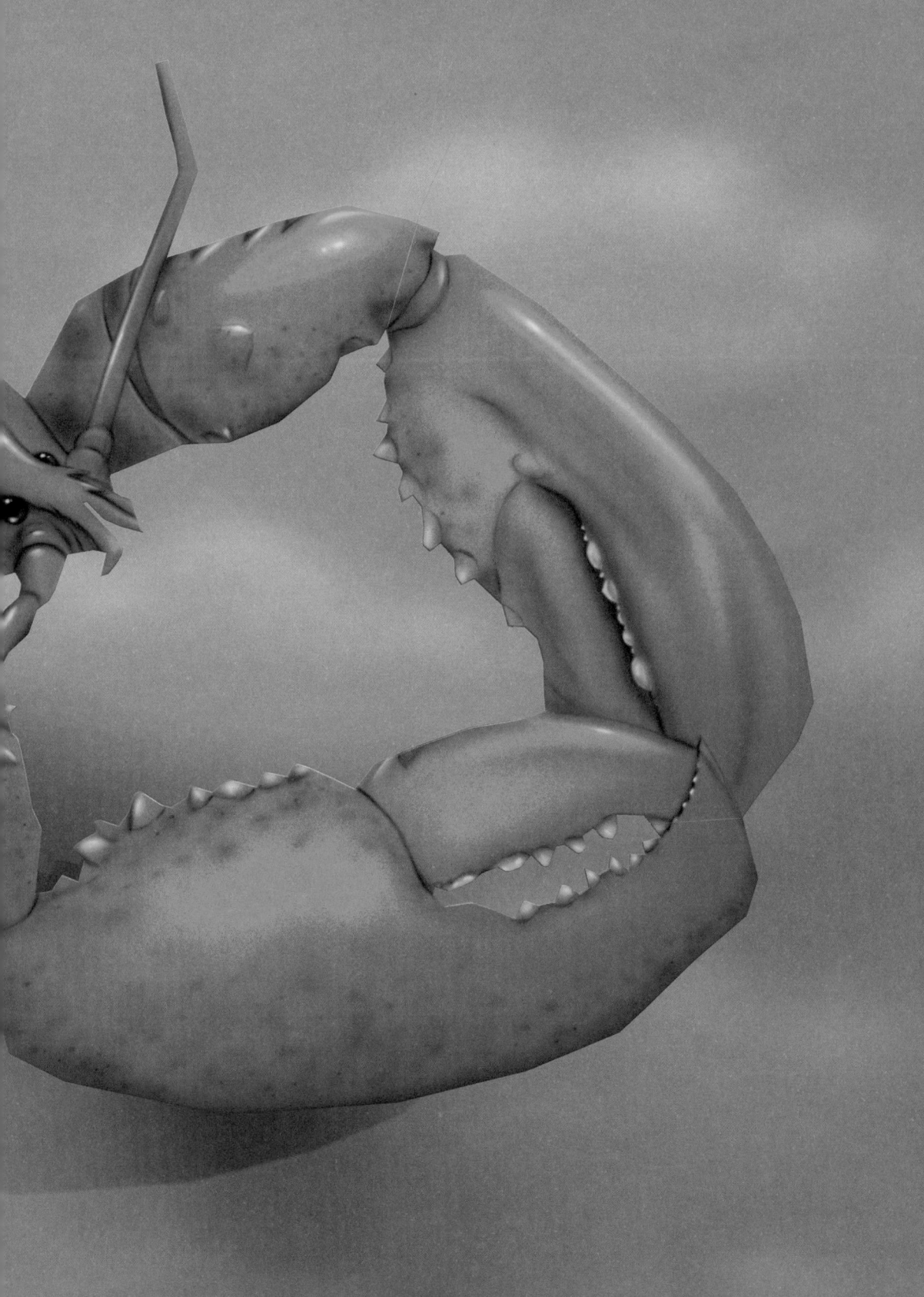

Opposite and overleaf: Farmhouse library at Deer Acres, with
Robert Venturi's "Tiffany" lamp, andirons, and furniture

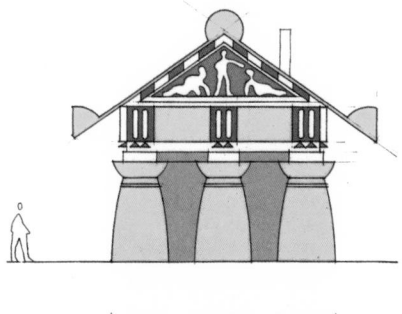 

Drawing of elevations of Eclectic House Series by Robert Venturi, 1977. The
drawing shows alternate elevations for a single plan.

Above: Temple shed at Deer Acres. Venturi re-imagines classical
architectural forms as decoration for the shed. Overleaf: Temple shed
at Deer Acres, front facade. The "temple" is purposefully revealed as a
false facade, casting shadows on the facade of the shed behind.

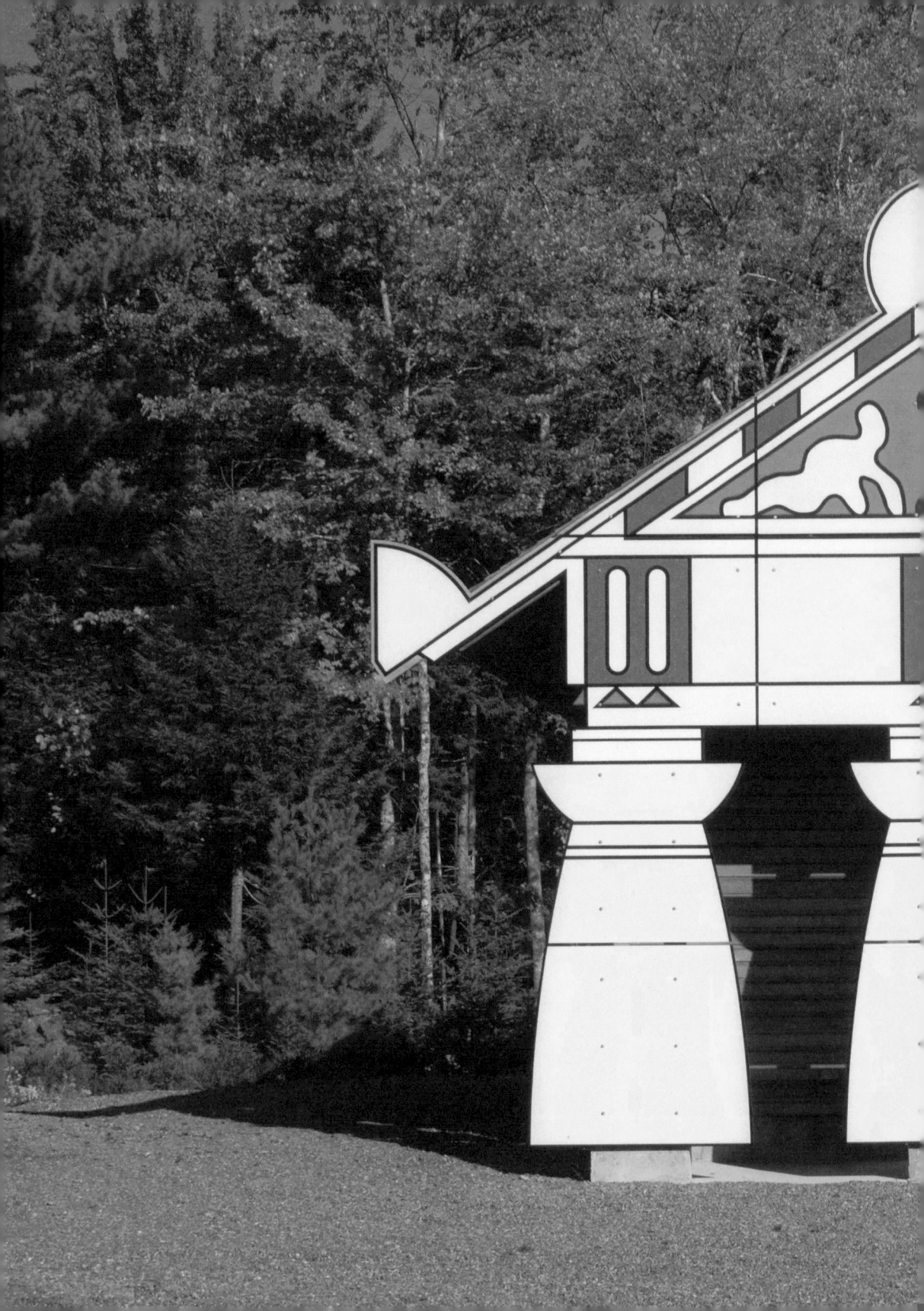

Pages 114–15: Flowers pattern variant by Steven Izenour for the Fabric
Workshop and Museum and A.S.A.P. Above: Best Panel garage at Deer
Acres. Overleaf and pages 120–21: Best Panel garage at Deer Acres.
Detail of porcelain-enameled steel panels produced for Best Products
Company showroom, Langhorne, Pennsylvania, 1973–79. Removed
from the original building in 2005

ACKNOWLEDGMENTS

The author would like to acknowledge that the conception and construction of the buildings at A.S.A.P. would not have been possible without the contributions of a multitude of talented individuals. First and foremost, it gives me the greatest of pleasure to thank Robert Venturi, Denise Scott Brown, and Steve Izenour, principals at Venturi, Scott Brown and Associates, Inc. for their wonderfully inspired designs. Years of visits and conversations have produced buildings that embody the same sense of freedom and play that we try to achieve at A.S.A.P./Kippy's Kamp. The visions of these three architects could not have been achieved without the help of their staff, especially John Izenour and Lauren Jacobi.

I am especially grateful to former VSBA Associates, Tim Kearney and Claudia Cueto of CuetoKEARNEY Architects, and to Ron Evitts of Ronald Evitts Architect LLC (r.e.a.l.) for the special help he provided Bob Venturi and me. With incredible ingenuity and technical skill, artist Michael Wommack of Michael Wommack Studios created and matched special colors, while mechanical designer Steve Schultz of Electro Mechanical Systems cut and bent metal, each better than anyone I've ever met.

A million thanks are due to the ever-capable, best builder any of the architects said they had ever worked with, John Dargis, his right-hand man John Albee, and crew for taking VSBA's few detailed drawings and many more verbal ideas, and making them into real buildings.

Special thanks are owed to George Mansfield, John Clancy, and Dave Ruddy, who helped Steve Izenour and me begin the very first buildings at Shore Cottage with the glowing blue cook shack and brilliant yellow tent.

I am honored that Kathy Hiesinger, with her brilliant writing, intense accuracy, and thorough knowledge of the subject matter, has been generous enough to write this superb essay and assist with a million other things. She has been a long-time friend and collaborator, providing me with invaluable advice and enthusiastic support. I would also like to thank my dear cousin Patterson Sims; my right hand for many years, Stephanie Alison Greene; and Amy Wilkins for helping me with fond memories, historical facts, creative writing, and great enthusiasm for this complicated project.

Takaaki Matsumoto of Matsumoto Incorporated has, as usual, produced a marvelous design for this book, and many others. Takaaki, along with Amy Wilkins and Hisami Aoki, never fails to create something logical and elegant from the mere kernel of an idea, in this case my desire to present VSBA's architecture in Maine.

Marion Boulton Stroud

The essayist would like to thank the following whose information and memories made this book possible, particularly Marion Boulton Stroud, John Izenour, and Robert Venturi, as well as Claudia Cueto, John Dargis, Kathryn E. Higgins, Lauren Jacobi, Timothy P. Kearney, and Michael Wommack, all having read the text in an earlier version. I am additionally grateful to Kathryn E. Higgins for surveying all the documents and images provided by VSBA, A.S.A.P., and the FWM. Special thanks are owed to Joseph McDermott for so patiently preparing the manuscript.

Kathryn Bloom Hiesinger

Venturi, Scott Brown and Associates, Inc. would like to acknowledge the work of so many staff members and associated architects that made the lively buildings at A.S.A.P. possible:

VSBA staff: Robert Venturi, Denise Scott Brown, Steven Izenour with Tony Bracali, Stephen van Dyck, Lauren Jacobi, John Izenour, David Marohn, and Andy Pasonic.

Special thanks to Tim Kearney and Claudia Cueto of CuetoKEARNEYdesign Architects, Ron Evitts of Ronald Evitts Architects LLC (r.e.a.l.), Steve Schultz of Electro Mechanical Systems, and Michael Wommack.

Thanks to the ever capable John Dargis and his team of builders for taking our sketch designs and making real buildings from them.

And most particularly, thanks to everyone at A.S.A.P. who made the visits and conversations possible.

And last but not least, all of our gratitude to Kippy, the presiding genius of A.S.A.P. for the inspiration and opportunity she provided.

Attributions for individual projects:
A-frame for Art, Deer Acres, T-shirt house, Flowers tent: design: Steven Izenour with Tim Kearney; fabrication: Electro Mechanical Systems; painting: Michael Wommack. *Temple shed*: design: Robert Venturi with Tim Kearney; fabrication: Electro Mechanical Systems; painting: Michael Wommack. *Palette house*: design: Steven Izenour (VSBA), Tim Kearney and Claudia Cueto (CuetoKEARNEYdesign Architects); fabrication: Electro Mechanical Systems; painting: Michael Wommack. *Best Panel garage*: design: Tim Kearney (CuetoKEARNEYdesign Architects); Robert Venturi with David Marohn (VSBA); fabrication: Electro Mechanical Systems. *Flower house*: design: Ronald Evitts (r.e.a.l); Denise Scott Brown and Robert Venturi (VSBA); with Jonathan Ho (r.e.a.l.).

Robert Venturi and Denise Scott Brown

THE ACADIA SUMMER ARTS PROGRAM

The Acadia Summer Arts Program—commonly referred to as A.S.A.P., Kippy's Kamp, and Kamp Kippy—is an internationally known summer artists' residency located in breathtaking Acadia National Park, on Mount Desert Island, Maine. Since 1993 the program has furnished invitees with the time, space, and resources to rejuvenate their creative practices. Each year, A.S.A.P. convenes an impressive array of artists and arts professionals, including museum directors, curators, architects, painters, sculptors, filmmakers, musicians, poets, dancers, and historians. The island is dotted with A.S.A.P.'s private cottages, which guests are free to use as either peaceful work space or for simple rest and relaxation. Most of the guests' time is unstructured, but the program provides weekly communal activities—dinners, guest lectures, and boat excursions to the surrounding islands—and annual public events such as exhibitions, film screenings, dance performances, and concerts.

Marion "Kippy" Boulton Stroud, the founder of A.S.A.P., has had a lifelong passion for supporting and facilitating artistic production. In 1977 she founded the Fabric Workshop and Museum in Philadelphia, where she currently serves as artistic director. Having spent summers on Mount Desert Island since childhood, Kippy wanted to share the beautiful Maine landscape with her friends and colleagues. Beginning as a small gathering in Kippy's coastal home, Shore Cottage, the program has blossomed into a summer-long influx of more than three hundred guests each year. Consequently, the physical space has evolved into a complex of studios, offices, and lecture facilities, designed by Robert Venturi, Denise Scott Brown, and the late Steven Izenour of Venturi, Scott Brown and Associates. Despite this growth, the intimate, familial quality of A.S.A.P. remains.

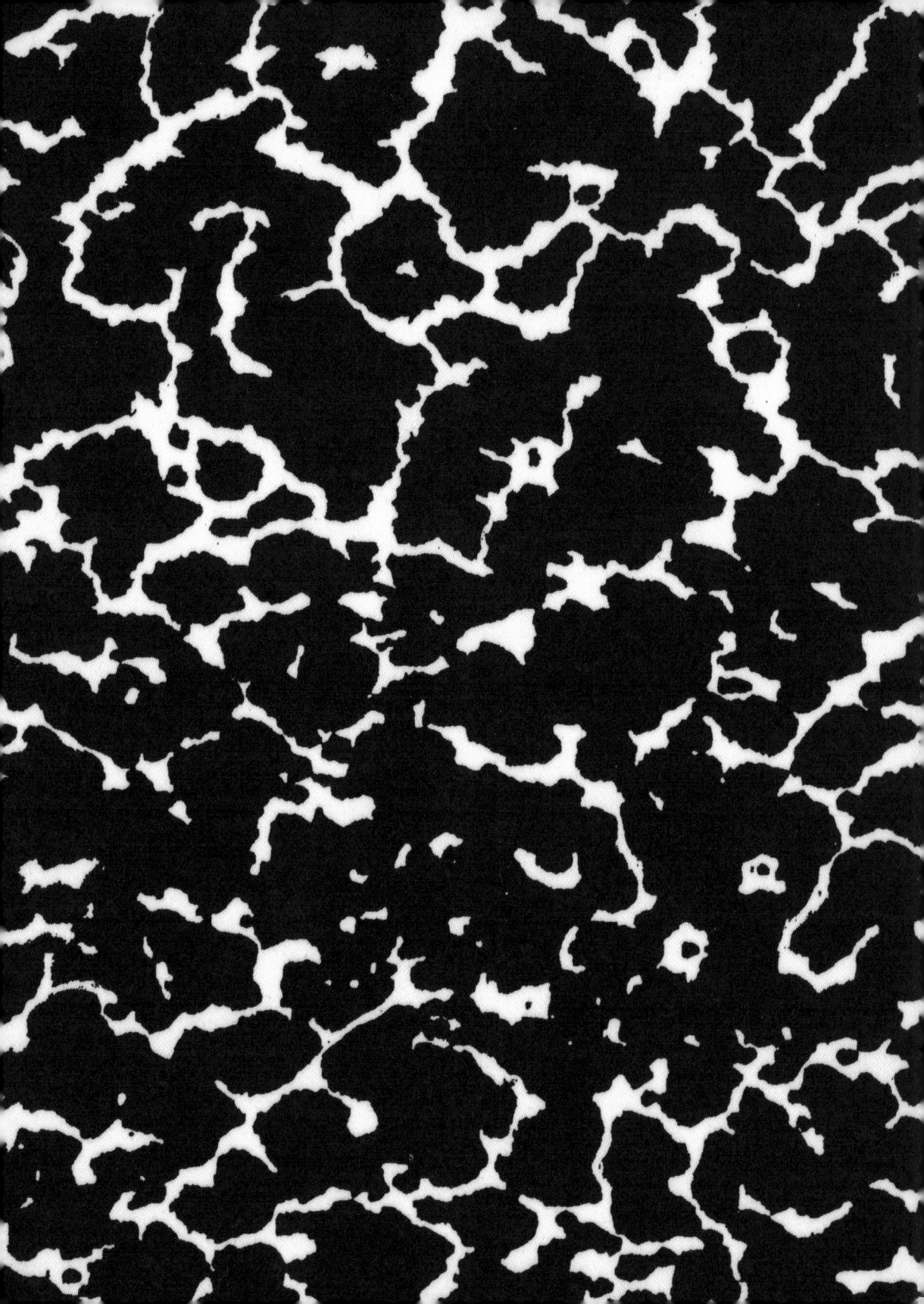